Public Administration

ANNALS OF PUBLIC ADMINISTRATION

Editor-in-Chief

JACK RABIN

Rider College
Lawrenceville, New Jersey

MARGARET ROSE, Assistant to the Editor-in-Chief

Managing Editors

GERALD J. MILLER   W. BARTLEY HILDRETH

University of Kansas   Kent State University
Lawrence, Kansas   Kent, Ohio

Topic Areas

A complete listing of editors' affiliations and editorial boards can be found at the end of this volume.

Bureaucracy / Jack Rabin, Editor
Criminal Justice Administration / William A. Jones, Jr., Editor
Health and Human Resources Administration / Robert Agranoff, Editor
Implementation / Frank Thompson, Editor
Intergovernmental Relations / Richard H. Leach, Editor
Organization Management / Chester A. Newland, Editor
Policy Formulation and Evaluation / G. Ronald Gilbert, Editor
Public Administration Education / Thomas Vocino, Editor
Public Administration History and Theory / Joseph A. Uveges, Jr., Editor
Public Budgeting and Financial Management / Thomas Lynch, Editor
Public Personnel Administration and Labor Relations / David H. Rosenbloom, Editor
Regulation and Administrative Law / Victor Rosenblum, Editor
Research Methods in Public Administration / Frank P. Scioli, Jr., Editor

Volume 1. Public Administration: History and Theory in Contemporary Perspective, edited by Joseph A. Uveges, Jr.

(other volumes in preparation)

Public Administration

History and Theory
in Contemporary Perspective

Edited by
JOSEPH A. UVEGES, Jr.
Western Kentucky University
Bowling Green, Kentucky

Marcel Dekker, Inc.
New York and Basel

Library of Congress Cataloging in Publication Data
Main entry under title:
Public administration, history and theory in con-
    temporary perspective.

    (Annals of public administration, ISSN 0278-4289;
1.   Public administration history and theory)
    Includes indexes.
    Contents: The changing patterns of public administra-
tion theory in America / Richard J. Stillman II—The
theory and practice of public administration as a
science of the artifactual / Vincent Ostrom—Toward
democracy within and through administration Robert T.
Golembiewski—[etc.]
    1. Public administration—Addresses, essays,
lectures. 2. Public administration—Addresses, essays,
lectures. I. Uveges, Joseph Andrew. II. Series.
III. Series: Annals of public administration.   Public
administration history and theory.
JF1351.P817   350   81-19428
ISBN 0-8247-1557-8   AACR2

MARCEL DEKKER, INC.
270 Madison Avenue, New York, New York 10016

Current printing (last digit):
10 9 8 7 6 5 4 3 2 1

Printed in the United States of America

About the Series

The Annals of Public Administration is designed to present issues of topical concern to the public administration community. The series bring together the efforts of several hundred scholars and practitioners in twelve topic areas of public administration.

The goal of the Annals, therefore, is to encourage the most widespread dissemination of ideas. All volumes will be the product of the interaction between a topic-area editor for each topic area and a group of experts serving as both editorial board and as advisors.

The topic areas to be covered in the Annals are:

1. Criminal Justice Administration
2. Health and Human Resources Administration
3. Implementation
4. Intergovernmental Relations
5. Organization Management
6. Policy Formulation and Evaluation
7. Public Administration Education
8. Public Administration History and Theory
9. Public Budgeting and Financial Management
10. Public Personnel Administration and Labor Relations
11. Regulation and Administrative Law
12. Research Methods in Public Administration

Because the series tries to remain up to date on current issues and topics in the field, it is quite important for the editor-in-chief and the topic-area editors to receive feedback from readers. What is your evaluation of the ways in which authors have approached the issues covered in a particular volume? What topics do you foresee will become important issues for the profession in the future? Please address your remarks to the topic-area editor and/or editor-in-chief.

We hope that the *Annals of Public Administration* will fulfill its goal and become a useful tool for the public administration community.

Jack Rabin

Preface

To enter into a discussion of public administration history and theory is to step headlong into a search for disciplinary identity. Although significant questions as to the existence of a "discipline" of public administration remain unresolved, one point is obvious. Any ultimate determination will be based on the past, present, and future directions taken in the study and practice of public administration.

Theory and history tend to converge when one seeks to identify a coherent body of knowledge for public administration. Students must seek to provide a systematic record and analysis of events crucial to the ways in which public administration has developed as an academic and professional field. In addition, efforts must continue to communicate data and sets of propositions about causal factors and future trends in the development of public administration. That other recognized disciplines have had to cope with similar necessities and problems has not prevented those disciplines from gaining recognition and acceptance.

The effort underway through the publication of the *Annals of Public Administration* represents only one of many recent attempts to expand the exchange of knowledge and values among those who have academic and professional interests in public administration. No fewer than 20 international, national, and regional journals with public administration as their primary focus are available as of 1981. Memberships in the American Society for Public Administration (ASPA) and the National Association of Schools of Public Affairs and Administration (NASPAA) continue to grow, with particular emphasis on individual and institutional involvement. Regional units within ASPA continue to expand their academic and professional activities in addition to their roles within the national organization. In addition, 1980 marked the initiation of the full implementation of NASPAA's *peer review process,* which seeks to provide for the systematic, yet voluntary, review of professional master's-level public administration programs. Efforts continue within NASPAA for the consideration of similar processes for baccalaureate degree programs. Thus, from the perspective of the availability of research literature, large-scale national identity through professional and academic organizations, and curricular development, public administration is alive and prospering.

The topics public administration history and theory are but two of many topical concerns to be addressed within the series *Annals of Public Administration.* Any or all of the topic areas to be developed in the annals are themselves complex and ever changing. In this volume we seek only to provide an overview of the depth and breadth of public administration history and theory and to treat a few major issues that seem to persistently appear.

Joseph A. Uveges, Jr.

Contributors

Buford L. Brinlee Department of Political Science and Sociology, University of North Florida, Jacksonville, Florida

Luther F. Carter Department of Political Science, College of Charleston, Charleston, South Carolina

Miriam Ershkowitz Department of Political Science, Temple University, Philadelphia, Pennsylvania

Robert T. Golembiewski Department of Political Science, University of Georgia, Athens, Georgia, *and* Faculty of Management, University of Calgary, Calgary, Alberta, Canada

Vincent Ostrom Workshop in Political Theory and Policy Analysis, *and* the Department of Political Science, Indiana University, Bloomington, Indiana

Laurence J. O'Toole, Jr. Department of Political Science, Auburn University, Auburn, Alabama

Daniel M. Poore * Master of Public Administration Program, The Pennsylvania State University, Capitol Campus, Middletown, Pennsylvania

Richard J. Stillman II Public Affairs Department, George Mason University, Fairfax, Virginia

*Mr. Poore is currently affiliated with Coastal Carolina College, University of South Carolina, Conway, South Carolina.

Contents

Part 1

Democratic and Bureaucratic Theories in Transition: Trends toward a Common Professional Focus

Although most efforts to identify public administration as an independent entity focus on the seminal work of Wilson in his essay "The Study of Administration" [1], public administration history and theory in the United States begin much earlier. In Chapter 1 Professor Richard Stillman develops the point that the basic patterns for public administration theory were already taking shape in the essays and statements of the Founding Fathers. Building upon a theme addressed earlier by Herbert Kaufman in "The Emerging Conflicts in the Doctrines of Public Administration" [2], Stillman suggests that for a time each of three basic administrative patterns dominated the domestic conceptions of public administration theory. Current problems regarding an identity for public administration, he suggests, result from a confusion of roles and expectations for public administration brought about by the convergence of all three of the basic patterns. The difference, however, between the current identity dilemma and those of the past is that while in the past it was possible for one of the three patterns to dominate an era, in today's world of public administration more of a "standoff" has occurred.

Other kinds of ongoing debates within public administration that characterize the field include the question of the linkages between theory and practice in public administration and the relation of values and organizational structure and behavior. In Chapter 2 Professor Vincent Ostrom treats these questions and their relationship to the development of public administration identity. He questions some basic assumptions about the manner in which the practice of public administration is approached. Emphasizing a valuational mode rather than an application of natural science methods, he elevates the role of human values and variations in the ongoing organizational environment. He suggests that the reliance upon traditional authoritarian organizational modes produces effects on individuals that are counter to their own as well as the organization's interests. Multiple levels of meaning require that public administration remain open to various kinds of knowledge, skill, and interest.

Another long-standing debate of paramount importance within the discipline is the question of democratic values versus bureaucratic values. Much attention and many pages of research have been devoted to the issue of whether or not a democratic society is enhanced or hindered by the organization and operation of the bureaucratic model. According to Professor Robert Golembiewski (Chapter 3), the effort to put bureaucratic principles in the service of republican democracy is subject to question.

Clearly the efficacy of bureaucracy for attaining democratic values is under attack. Many theoretical and practical efforts have been made since the 1960s to provide greater direct citizen access to the bureaucratic process. The merit system itself has come under more careful scrutiny, in particular its ability to provide for adaptation in governmental personnel recruitment and selection. The need for executive leadership (the Watergate fiasco notwithstanding) has led to the initiation of merit-system reforms in the areas of recruitment, pay, promotion, and retention of senior executives and to efforts to provide for merit-based rewards.

For the most part, however, these efforts have addressed bureaucratic problems from a more or less external orientation. Golembiewski suggests that the problems that confront administrative organizations must be dealt with by efforts to reorient and restructure the organizational setting to provide for greater utilization of existing personnel and experience. By addressing the problems that attend the actual work units within the bureau, he seeks to energize the latent power of members of the bureau in order to increase efficiency and reduce costs. By suggesting that Organization Development (OD) theory and practice is one means for achieving those objectives, he provides an organizational mode more highly consistent with democratic values.

In Chapters 1 through 3 one theme appears to be consistently evident. Most efforts to fashion a basic identity for public administration seek to resolve the following questions: How do we identify our basic democratic values, and under which mode of organizational structure and individual behavior are those values most likely to be achieved? Obviously, the answers are not so easily codified.

So long as preparation for a career in the public sector was dictated by one's own academic or professional interests, the preceding questions were left to the individual to ponder and resolve. As any one dominant pattern emerged, it brought with it certain expectations regarding the "proper" preparation for administrative careers in the public sector. However, as the scope of the role of government began to change as a result of growing demands for government services during the Depression and immediately after World War II, so also did the concern for a more rigorous effort to provide for a better prepared public manager. The period of the 1950s and 1960s was a testing ground for new and often unacceptable ideas about the need to develop a common professional focus for public officials in managerial roles. Little common ground could be found upon which to develop such a focus; it would take not only open dialogue among public administration academic and professional leaders but also the emergence of a new national organization committed to the development of high-quality academic curricula for the education of public administration professionals.

The National Association of Schools of Public Affairs and Administration (NASPAA), as this new organization was named, established membership on an institutional, rather than individual, basis. The focus of NASPAA was on strengthening institutional curricula and promoting the flow of information regarding public administration programs among its member institutions. As a result, growing support materialized for the discussion of the need to provide a more coherent format for public administration professional programs. In Chapter 4 Professor Daniel Poore discusses not only the debates that marked this period but also the essential characteristics of the *disciplinary identity* to be sought in master's-level programs.

Of special note are the NASPAA standards. Careful, considered judgments were made in constructing the matrix of subject matters. Of concern with regard to the thrust of public administration history and theory, given the previous chapters in this volume, is the effort to integrate democratic values and modes of behavior throughout each of the subject matter areas. Thus although the standards do not mandate certain "required" courses or technical skills, they do make clear the decision that democratic values and their implementation should be related to all areas of substantive or academic learning. It should also be noted that NASPAA's efforts in identifying curricular needs include a set of "Guidelines and Standards for Baccalaureate Degree Programs" [3], which is an area of great interest and growth in public administration education. Although the focus for each level of program is different, most of the basic concerns regarding program integration of values and skills remain intact.

It should be clear by this point that the issues regarding public administration identity have not been resolved in this volume. Rather the chapters presented should provide a systematic basis for discussion and ongoing efforts to learn more about where we are, how we got here, and where we should be going in public administration in the future. The editor, of course, takes full responsibility for the selection of the material in this volume; the extent to which it is useful to students of public administration will be determined by each reader.

References

1. Woodrow Wilson, "The Study of Administration," *Political Science Quarterly*, June, 1887, pp. 197–222.
2. Herbert Kaufman, "Emerging Conflicts in the Doctrines of Public Administration," *The American Political Science Review*, 50 (December 1956): 1057–1073.
3. *Guidelines and Standards for Baccalaureate Degree Programs in Public Affairs/Public Administration*, National Association of Schools of Public Affairs and Administration, Washington, D.C., 1976.

1

The Changing Patterns of Public Administration Theory in America

Richard J. Stillman II
George Mason University,
Fairfax, Virginia

*Defining Public Administration—its boundaries, scope, and substance—
has been a central, perhaps the central, preoccupation of administrative
theorists since the field's conscious emergence as a scholarly enterprise a
century ago. Within the last decade the field's "identity crisis," as Dwight
Waldo once labeled the dilemma, has become especially acute as a plethora
of models, approaches, and theories now abound in Public Administration. The author of this chapter reexamines the writings of the Founding
Fathers and finds three basic patterns of Public Administration implicit in
political philosophies of Hamilton, Jefferson, and Madison. The author
argues that since the inception of the United States each of these basic administrative patterns—i.e., Hamiltonian classicism, Jeffersonian roman-
iticism, and Madisonian neoclassicism—has at one time or another, to a
large extent, dominated our conception of Public Administration theory.
Much of our current definitional confusion regarding Public Administration theory is due to the sudden and simultaneous reappearance of all three
administrative patterns in competition with one another as the way to
understand the field.*

In *The Creation of the American Republic 1776–87* [1], Gordon Wood
argues that the enduring significance of the American Revolution was the
transformation of Western political authority from the medieval European
tradition of sovereignty derived from the three *social orders*—crown,

lords, and commons—to a single, unified basis of popular rule. This dramatic and sudden shift in the conception of political authority posed, however, special dilemmas for government administration. For centuries in Western Europe *public administrators* had been the direct agents of the crown. Whom would public administrators now serve in a new liberal society? Would public administration* find a place in a government without a crown?

Despite the absence of reference to Public Administration in the U.S. Constitution, the Founding Fathers gave the subject considerable thought and reflection in many of their letters, pamphlets, and other public documents. Granted, the topic of liberty, not administration, received the most detailed attention and ardent praise from that generation of revolutionaries. Their perilous wartime experience coupled with the turbulent economic and political instability under the Articles of Confederation only confirmed in the minds of many that effective execution of the public interest must be concomitant with the pursuit of their hard-won liberties from George III and the British Parliment. In the crisis decade of the 1770s, many saw firsthand how enjoyment of personal liberty was, indeed, predicated upon effective execution of public policy in general and its administration in particular. As with most critical issues that confronted these literate and gifted men, however, the framers of the U.S. Constitution were hardly of one mind relative to the nature and substance of Public Administration in America. Indeed, their views on this subject, gained from their wide-ranging public service and exhaustive readings of Western political thinkers, were sharply divergent and, to a large extent, directly derived from the following: first, their views of the nature of man; second, their attitudes toward political authority; and third, the notions about the role of government in society. From the writings of the Founding Fathers, three schools of administrative thought evolved that today still profoundly influence the basic patterns of Public Administration in America.

Alexander Hamilton and the Classical Administration Pattern

Of all the Founding Fathers, none displayed more enthusiasm for administrative theory and practice than Alexander Hamilton. Hamilton was truly

---

*The author follows Dwight Waldo's practice of using lowercase letters for *public administration* when referring to the actual government phenomenon and capitalizing *Public Administration* when referring to the study of or ideas about this phenomenon.

a man of executive action from the time of his service as the brilliant 23-year-old aide-de-camp to General Washington in the Revolution to his masterful planning, control, and development of national finances as the first Secretary of Treasury in President Washington's Cabinet.

As Leonard D. White wrote, "In the *Federalist Papers* Hamilton set out the first systematic exposition of Public Administration, a contribution which stood alone for generations. In his public life, he displayed a capacity for organization, system, leadership which after a century and a half is hardly equaled" [2]. White's glowing praise of Hamiltonian administrative theory and practice may have been exaggerated due to the relative proximity of both men's views on the subject, yet certainly fitting honor belongs to Hamilton in that he alone gave the most "conscious" attention to this field throughout his prolific writings and active national public service.

The dominant theme in Hamilton's concept of Public Administration was his ardent and enthusiastic nationalism. His was a big, broad, bold image of America as a national power politically, economically, and militarily. His writings were replete with expressions of glowing admiration for the promotion of the "public interest," "public good," "good of the general society," "common interest," "national interest," and "true interest of the community." There was nothing modest or timid about Hamilton's proposed public projects to promote commerce and industry; create a professionalized Army and Navy; establish a national bank, a national university, and public school systems; and create national public work projects such as building ships, roads, canals, and dams and mining precious metals.

Hamilton favored strong, effective, action-oriented government, not only to engage in multiple developmental plans, but also because he held a dim, almost Hobbesian view of human nature. Strong public institutions, according to Hamilton, were necessary to protect human liberty—or, put more bluntly, to protect us from each other. As Hamilton wrote [3]:

> In government framed for durable liberty, no less regard must be paid to giving the magistrate a proper degree of authority to make and execute the laws with rigor, than guarding against the encroachment upon the rights of the community. As too much power leads to despotism, too little leads to anarchy, and both eventually to the ruin of the people.

Effective public authority, in short, was necessary to protect us from our own prevailing passions, ambitions, and interests. This pessimistic assessment of humanity hardly endeared Hamilton to most of his countrymen then or since. Some have even suggested, perhaps cruelly, that "Hamilton loved his country more than his fellow countrymen." Whatever others have thought of Hamilton's tough-minded realism, his conception of human nature coupled with his notions about an expanded role for government led him, at least in comparison with other Founding Fathers, to diminished concern with the external form of government. Rather, his interests focused on what he liked to refer to as the "tone of government." For Hamilton, in the words of Clinton Rossiter, "tone was legitimacy, competence, dignity, authority, and in one word 'energy.' The absence of tone was caprice, contumacy mistrust, atrophy, in one word 'weakness' "[4].

Thus, no wonder, given Hamilton's predilection for strong, effective, "energetic" government, his *classical theory* of Public Administration was logically framed with that specific end in mind:

1. An enlarged, "conscious," active role for administration characterized by *energy* and *leadership* and *tone*
2. Administration unified as a process, with responsibility for administrative actions undivided and preferably concentrated in one individual (as opposed to being divided among members of a board or committee)
3. Administrative power allocated commensurate with the responsibility for administrative functions
4. Adequate duration in office to ensure administrative effectiveness and stability
5. Preference decidedly favoring paid, trained professionals (as opposed to part-time, unpaid volunteers) to staff administrative positions
6. Special emphasis on the economic and institutional requisites of administration (i.e., fiscal and military matters) as the necessary lifeblood for maintaining energetic and effective government

Thomas Jefferson and the Romantic Administrative Pattern

If a lusty nationalism fired Hamilton's political and administrative perspectives, concern for The People colored Jefferson's political outlook as well as administrative theory. Jefferson's writings, like Rousseau's, are salted with praise for homogenous mankind, The People. Perhaps this genuflection to individual liberty and to the advancement of mankind was never symbolized better than by Jefferson's pithy Preamble to the Declaration of Independence. Historian Wilson Carey McWilliams astutely observes [5]:

Jefferson believed in and was devoted to human progress. . . . If humanity was to move to higher things, it would be on the foundations created by good men. The political order was designed to develop and improve man as a moral being without which all progress would be hollow.

Jefferson's utopian meliorism for mankind, however, was set in a distinctly rural environment. The Jeffersonian vision of America was framed bucolically and peopled principally with sturdy, rustic yeomen. America, unlike crowded, urbanized, and despotic Europe, would remain free so long as government was popularly supported and rurally based. Typical of the pastoral image that flashes throughout his prolific writings is the following comment [6]:

> I think our governments will remain virtuous for many centuries; as long as they are chiefly agricultural; and this will be as long as there shall be vacant lands in any part of America. When they get piled up one upon another in large cities, as in Europe, they will become corrupt as in Europe.

Unlike Hamilton, Jefferson exhibits a profound Enlightenment belief in human nature and the possibilities for its growth and perfection. Further, the people were the *one* interest, *one* will, and *the one* sovereign in society; the source of legitimate power; and the only "safe" depository for governmental authority. The people also were the only true purpose for which government should be erected: "The only orthodox object of the institution of government is to secure the greatest degree of happiness possible to the general mass of those associated under it" [7].

Whereas Hamilton spoke of governmental "authority," "responsibility," and "discretion," Jefferson emphasized, as Lynton K. Caldwell observed [8] the "limits on government" and the maximization of "individual rights," "liberty," and the "popular pursuit of happiness." Paradoxically, though, Hamilton was the one who charted the bold course for the governmental role in society to promote the "public good," whereas Jefferson, aside from his enthusiasm for public education, defined limited government as "the best government": "I am for government that is frugal and simple," he stressed repeatedly. Jefferson also emphasized the importance of keeping government as close to the "grass roots" as possible. The New England town meeting was his "ideal" democratic institution. Jefferson heaped scorn on his opponents, the Federalists, for the "extravagancy" and "complexity" and "distance" from the people which they sought to promulgate in government.

Based on the Jeffersonian vision of a rurally based, popularly supported, and limited government, a very different *romantic pattern* of Public Administration emerges from his pen, significantly different at least in comparison with the classical Hamiltonian model:

1. Extensive popular participation, especially mass voluntaristic involvement in administration (as opposed to paid, full-time professionals)
2. Maximum decentralization in order to limit administration and bring it as close as possible under the scrutiny of *The People*
3. Emphasis on *simplicity* and *economy* of administrative actions—simplicity so that administrative actions could be understood by the average citizen and economy in order to avoid the "sins" of extravagance and waste in government
4. Stress placed upon strict legal limitations of administrative authority in order to prevent possible transgressions on individual liberties by autocratic magistrates
5. Limits on the range of administrative activities, so that the role of the administrator constitutes a narrow functional specialist (rather than a broadly trained and broadly ranging professional)
6. Issue orientation focused upon protection of individual rights, limitation of administrative actions, and promotion of participation in public affairs through popular education

James Madison and the Neoclassical Administrative Pattern

James Madison shared Jefferson's enthusiasm for an agrarian-based society, principally because Madison believed that a homogeneous society would reduce potential "tensions" and "strains" in the social fabric of the polity. Madison, however, differed from his fellow Virginian's idealization of the broad abstraction *The People* because of what he believed was its "prescriptive" appeal rather than "descriptive" accuracy.

The bedrock of Madisonian analysis of America's politics was, instead, the *faction* (or in modern terms, *interest group*), which he saw as the chief "fount" of political activity in America. Madison's often-quoted definition of *faction* in *Federalist 10* indicates that while he saw factions as prime movers of American politics, he exhibited little liking for any sort of faction [9]:

> a number of citizens, whether amounting to a majority or a minority of the whole, who are united and actuated by some common impulse or passion, or of interests, adverse to the rights of other citizens, or the permanent and aggregate interests of the community.

The persistence of factions in American politics was, for Madison, rooted in the very nature of man. Madison was very much the sober realist about the "two-sided" character of mankind—i.e., capable of greatness, charity, and virtue but equally passionate, self-interested, and self-willed. This complex diversity of human nature produced a complex diversity of interest groups in society. Man was inclined to seek others of like interests and pursue those interests, even to the detriment of others. Unlike Marxian analysis which concludes that the basic conflict in a capitalistic society is between the propertyless and the propertied, Madisonian analysis, anticipating modern behavioralists by nearly 150 years, categorizes a wide variety of interest groups in society. For example, Madison pointed out the various agricultural interest groups in his native Virginia alone: "In one district, the chief products were Indian corn and cotton; in another, the tobacco and wheat; in still another, chiefly wheat, rye, and livestock." The subject of slavery, he observed, divided east and west Virginia, and in some communities factions were divided over "the great and agitating subjects of roads and water and communications." As he told the Constitutional Convention in 1787, "We cannot be regarded even at this time as one homogeneous mass, in which everything that affects a part will in the same manner affect the whole" [10].

In viewing America as a faction-based nation, James Madison, in the words of Samuel P. Huntington, conceived that "American society was heterogeneous, fluid, and evolving. The only permanent fact was the inevitability of factions. The particular composition and strength of factions never remained stable" [11]. In recognition of this continual, frantic social flux, the Madisonian concept of government was essentially that of a balancing mechanism, i.e., a sort of mediator among contending factions. Since factions could not realistically be eliminated in society without enormous costs to human liberty, their worst side effects could at best be controlled only through institutional devices. His fundamental advice in *Federalist 51* on the framing of a stable and enduring government was "Ambition must be made to counteract ambition" so that by this means "you must first enable the government to control the governed; in the next place, oblige it to control itself." Thus, his argument for adequacy of constitutional checks and balances follows, also in *Federalist 51* [12]:

> We see it particularly displayed in all of the subordinate distributions of power, where the constant aim is to divide and arrange the several offices in such a manner as that each may be a check on the other—that the private interest of every individual may be sentinel over the public rights.

Historian Ralph Ketcham observes a strong predilection for the Aristotelian Golden Mean throughout Madison's writings—with interest balancing interest; state and local prerogatives balancing national interests; and executive, judicial, and legislative interests balancing each other. As Ketcham writes [13]:

> As he [Madison] saw repeatedly how concentration of power inclined toward tyranny or the triumph of selfish interests, his devotion to checks and balances and the doctrine of separation of power increased. He disliked the legislative dominance in the Virginia Constitution almost as much as he had the executive domination of the deposed royal government. Each resulted in foolishness and injustice. To Madison, however, separation of powers did not mean paralysis of powers. He ridiculed the impotent office of the governor created by the Virginia Constitution, and he scorned the incapacity of the general government under the Articles of Confederation. His zeal for an efficient government at all levels arose from his frustration he felt in seeking to do the things necessary to fulfill the revolution.

In his attempt to "fulfill the revolution," Madison discovered the idea of the *extended republican form of government*, which perhaps places Madison alongside the truly original and distinguished theorists in Western political thought. Madison showed how a large heterogeneous society, such as the United States, could "balance" competing interests in order to protect individual liberty and at the same time promote national interest more effectively than could small homogeneous city states (which in that day were considered the only safe havens for democracy). Only a large society of diverse interests represented by proper balance within government would, in his view, reduce the dangers of "tyranny of the majority" and protect the interest of the minority at the same time. In fact, the larger the number of distinct interests in a society, argued Madison, the less likelihood that any single one would tend to dominate the others and hence the reduced possibility of producing a tyranny of the majority and the more potential that minority rights might be preserved.

While it is a mistake to suggest that Madison developed any explicit view of Public Administration, from what he says about the subject of the executive branch and the execution of public policy, coupled with his faction-based vision of society, one can find an implicit description of Public Administration that significantly differs from either the Hamiltonian or Jeffersonian model:

1. Administrative processes are *pluralistic*—i.e., they are rooted in representation of divergent, changing, factional interests in society, so that

administrative goals can be neither static nor singular but rather are process oriented and representative of social diversity.

2. Administrative processes are aimed principally at *balancing interests* through discussion, negotiations, and compromise in order to promote political consensus and social stability.

3. Administrative processes, though separated formally by functional differentiation, in practice share authority with each of three branches —executive, legislative, and judicial; in other words, administrative processes are not isolated from each branch of government but interact in a complicated and continual manner of *checks and balances*.

4. Administrative processes also involve complex and continuous interaction across federal, state, and local boundaries.

5. Administrators are practitioners of the *art of the possible*, whose roles principally entail the ongoing responsibilities of discussion, negotiation, compromise, and the promotion of *social consensus*.

6. Emphasis is focused less on specific policy issues but rather on the adequacy of institutional *checks and balances* to control abuses of factions, to safeguard minority rights from the potential tyranny of the majority, and to promote social harmony by means of achieving an effective equilibrium among competing factions.

Tables 1 and 2 summarize the divergent political and administrative views of the three Founding Fathers.

The Dominance of Romantic Jeffersonianism in the Nineteenth Century: Public Administration in a Society of Island Communities

If the Federalist party—the party of Washington, Hamilton, and John Adams with its "large view" of the national interest—had survived in power throughout the nineteenth century, no doubt a much different administrative theory and practice would have emerged in America, i.e., administration that was professionalized, activist, and executive centered. Instead, multiple and profound social changes, largely beyond the control of the Federalists, brought about their swift and complete demise.

First, the absence of a significant external threat to the United States, due mainly to this nation's unique geographic isolation, stimulated little demand for mass standing armies with highly differentiated bureaucratic structures. While in the same period Europe created its professionalized military, the chief element of the modern bureaucratic state, throughout

Table 1 Summary of Three Founding Fathers' Political Views

	Source of political authority	View of man	Government's role in society	Chief source of threat to polity	Means of achieving "good life"	Institutional emphasis	Favored administrative pattern
Hamilton	Nation	Realistic	Promote national economic growth and political strength	Weak national institutions	Strong, effective national leadership	Federal executive	Classical *high-energy* pattern
Jefferson	People	Perfectible	Secure popular agrarian republic	Tyranny of centralized ruler	Decentralized popular institutions (e.g., New England town meetings)	Grassroots democracy	Romantic *low-energy* pattern
Madison	Faction	Realistic–perfectible	Balancing mechanism to control harmful side effects of factions	Tyranny of the majority	Extended representative republic (i.e., United States)	Complex checks and balances	Neoclassical *social equilibrium* pattern

Table 2 Summary of Three Founding Fathers' Administrative Views

	Image of administrative process	Purpose of administration	Degree of administrative discretion	Degree of centralization vs. decentralization	Favored type of public service	Preferred administrator's style	Area of chief administrative concern
Hamilton's classical pattern	Unified process	Energetic promotion of national interest	Broad professional discretion	Adequate centralization so "power equates with responsibility"	Professional careerist	"Doer"	Fiscal–military issues
Jefferson's romantic pattern	Popular process	Strictly limited range of activities to "those people can't do themselves"	Constricted functional specialist	Maximum decentralization of authority to check its possible abuse	Informal voluntary cooperation at the grass roots	"Servant of the people"	Popular education to stimulate civic involvement
Madison's neoclassical pattern	Pluralistic process	Foster social equilibrium through group representation	Interdependent with activities of executive, legislative, & judicial branches	Balanced involvement with all three levels of government—federal, state, local	Process oriented; concerned with negotiation, discussion, & compromise	"Practitioner of the art of the possible"	Institutional checks and balances

the nineteenth century (except for the Civil War) America could rest its primary defense upon the Jeffersonian concept of *citizen soldiers* (mainly used for quelling small-scale Indian uprisings). Geographic accident permitted the United States the luxury of *not* building a Hamiltonian-type professionalized military cadre for over a century. West Point, though established in 1802, was not designed initially to produced a trained officer corps but rather to supply adequate numbers of engineers to build roads, bridges, and canals throughout the Far West—i.e., functional specialists necessary to meet specific popular needs (in the classic spirit of Jeffersonianism).

Second, throughout most of the 1800s 9 out of 10 Americans derived their livelihood directly or indirectly from the land. As farming was the chief national occupation, agrarian self-sufficiency prompted little support for public goods and services with the possible exception of demands for provision of adequate postal and transportation links to gain access to national and international markets. The lack of demand for much public service, at least on the federal level, was characterized by the fact that for nearly a century after President Washington's administration only one federal Cabinet-level department was created, the Interior Department in 1849. Even then, that department was established only to combine several previously existing agencies under one roof. Furthermore, 86 percent of the growth in number of federal employees from 4837 to 36,872 between 1816 and 1861 was due to the expansion of *one* department, the Post Office.

Third, not only were formal governmental functions limited, but what tasks were performed were for the most part simple. As Leonard White observed, one major federal department, the Post Office, was a system of "vast, repetitive, fixed and generally routine operations" [14]. Complexity of purpose and process, on the other hand, would perhaps have stimulated "conscious," differentiated, and complex administrative analysis. Public service agencies that were in practice both simple and single purpose could fit neatly into the simplified Jeffersonian formula for "good" administration.

Fourth, such simple operations could, also with relative ease, be conducted under the Jeffersonian maxim of popular participation in government by means of patronage on the inside and legislative oversight from the outside. With little detriment to the provision of public services, the "Whig Image" prevailed in this era, as Wilfred E. Binkley has noted. Throughout the nineteenth century the "Whig Image" viewed presidential power as subordinate to legislative and popular oversight. Not until the twentieth century did Theodore Roosevelt carve out a "stewardship" role for the presidency, with significant, activist, and autonomous executive

powers. Popular participation in government was enthroned, furthermore, in this century by the rapid extension of universal male suffrage during and after Jackson's presidency as well as by the increasing number of
public positions filled by the ballot box rather than by appointment. As
Herbert Kaufman has pointed out, this century saw the values of popular
representation in public administration overshadow other values such as
neutral competence and/or executive control [15].

Perhaps the most identifiable reason for the wholehearted adoption
of romantic Jeffersonian administrative perspectives by this era was the
community-based authority structure of the American polity. As Robert
Wiebe notes in his outstanding historical analysis *The Search for Order,
1877–1920* [16]:

> America during the 19th century was a society of island communities.
> Weak communication severely restricted the interaction among these
> islands and dispersed power to form opinion and enact public policy.
> Education, both formal and informal, inhibited specialization and dis-
> couraged the accumulation of knowledge. The heart of the American
> democracy was local autonomy. The century after France had devel-
> oped a reasonably efficient, centralized public administration; Ameri-
> cans could not even conceive of a managerial government. Almost all
> of a community's affairs were still arranged informally.

A graphic picture of decentralized, popularly based, informally arranged
administrative practice in nineteenth-century America is perhaps best captured by Alexis de Tocqueville's perceptive description [17]:

> In America the power that conducts the administration is far less
> regular, less enlightened, less skillful, but a hundred-fold greater than in
> Europe. In no other country in the world do the citizens make such exer-
> tions for the common weal. I know of no people who have established
> schools so numerous and efficacious, places of public worship better
> suited to the wants of the inhabitants, or roads kept in better repair.
> Uniformity or permanence of design, the minute arrangement of details
> and the perfection of administrative system must not be sought for in
> the United States; what we find is the presence of a power, which, if it is
> somewhat wild, is at least robust, and an existence checkered with acci-
> dents, indeed, but full of animation and effort.

De Tocqueville further comments on its unwritten, unconscious, and
temporal dimensions as follows: 'The public administration is, so to speak,
oral and traditional. . . . Little is committed to writing, and that little is
soon wafted away forever, like the leaves of the Sibyl, by the smallest
breeze.'

While romantic Jeffersonianism may have dominated nineteenth-century administrative theory and practice, traces of classical Hamiltonianism did appear in this century. Ironically, classical models of administration waxed most intensely, though briefly, inside hotbeds of Jeffersonian politics. The South, for one, both prior to and during the Civil War, developed highly professional practitioners of the art and science of warfare, due largely to the peculiar southern brand of feudal idealism combined with the very real external threats of northern invasion plus internal slave insurrection. Douglas Southall Freeman's three-volume *Lee's Lieutenants* [18] ably captures the "flower" of southern military professionalism at its finest and fullest. Another blossoming of Hamiltonian classicism occurred during the presidency of Andrew Jackson. As Matthew Crensen points out in his book *The Federal Machine* [19], Amos Kendall, Jackson's Postmaster General, created a system of depersonalized, specialized hierarchical bureaucratic governance primarily to "guarantee good behavior of civil servants."

Certainly the Madisonian faction-based model could also be found in this era. One pressure group that was particularly influential was the commercial interests promulgating passage of protective tarriff legislation; another was the farm block that pressed for cabinet status for the Department of Agriculture in 1889. However, the *conscious study* of interest group politics involving policy formulation inside and outside public administration would have to await the twentieth century.

The Classical Hamiltonian Pattern in the Twentieth Century: Conscious, Unified, and Energetic Public Administration in a Distended Society

The breakdown of the old nineteenth-century social order based on cohesive island communities across America came swiftly and suddenly prior to turn of the century. It occurred before most Americans could comprehend what had happened, or understand why, or cope adequately with such cataclysmic change.

Multiple influences were at work in creating the profound and prodigious convulsion in the national structure of public authority. Cities grew at a more rapid rate in the 20 years prior to 1900 than at any previous time, due mainly to the flood of immigrants from abroad and rural migration at home. Industrialization turned village hamlets into sprawling urban manufacturing centers almost overnight. Factories multiplied as mechanical inventions were spewed out at an unprecedented rate to satisfy voracious domestic and foreign consumer appetites. Isolated "islands of communities" across America were swiftly bound into a cohesive whole by an all-enveloping web of communication and transportation lines. Rail, road, telephone, and telegraph brought a new mobility of products and people heretofore unknown in the ordered, tranquil world of the nineteenth century. Moreover, after more than a century of unique isolation, America was thrust into the troubled waters of imperialistic expansionism by the short, though hardly "splendid," Spanish–American War. Later, the full-scale national mobilization required by U.S. involvement in World War I was to sound the death knell for the traditions local autonomy in America.

The turn of the century was truly a dizzying and tumultuous period. Americans accustomed to a serene, personal world of "village society" felt the very foundations beneath their feet cracking. No small wonder Frederick Jackson Turner's essay touched a raw nerve when he foretold ominous consequences of the "closing of the American frontier." The claustrophobic fears of a door slammed shut made many Americans anxious indeed about being sealed in from all sides by rising new impersonal "isms"—urbanism, industrialism, nationalism, unionism, internationalism, mechanisms.

As historian Robert Wiebe writes [16],

> Already by the 1870's the autonomy of the community was badly eroded. The illusion of authority, however, endured. Innumerable townsmen continued to assume that they could harness the forces of the world to the destiny of their community. That confidence, the system's final foundation, largely disappeared during the eighties and nineties in the course of a dramatic struggle to defend the independence of the community.
>
> Although no replacement stood at hand, the outlines of an alternative system rather quickly took shape early in the twentieth century. By contrast to the personal, informal ways of the community, the new scheme was derived from the regulative, hierarchical needs of urban-industrial life. Through rules with impersonal sanctions, it sought continuity and predictability in a world of endless change. It assigned far greater power to government—in particular to a variety of flexible administrative devices—it encouraged the centralization of authority.

In this severe crisis of authority, numerous short-term fads burst onto the political scene. Humbug solutions abounded in the 1880s and 1890s to "cure" the then-perceived ills afflicting society. Financial cured loomed especially large among the popular remedies—from impassioned cries to "maintain the gold standard" to equally fervent pleas for "silver." Certainly, it does not take deep Jungian analysis to perceive that these financial antidotes were symbols reflecting mass anxiety over rapidly fragmenting community life in quest of "order" and "wholeness." Conscious lashing out at such evils as "trusts," "booze," and "the boss" reflected a subconscious unease at impersonal social forces, out of control and threatening destruction of the familiar, personalized nineteenth-century world. Not surprisingly, the popular novel of the day was Edward Bellamy's *Looking Backward*, which conjured up visions of a wondrous mechanized utopia encompassing so many of the cardinal virtues individuals saw disappearing in that age—i.e., virtues of purity, unity, community, democracy, and order.

It was also no coincidence that the social fabric first began to strain or tear at the point at which classical Hamiltonian administrative patterns reemerged. Did classicism not project at least the image, if not the reality, of order in the midst of rapid social decay? No doubt this is why a young Woodrow Wilson, after writing his popular treatise *Congressional Government*, which attacked the fragmented and irresponsible committee system in Congress, would turn immediately thereafter and pen a prophetic essay on the subject of Public Administration in this country in which he argued that Public Administration as a self-conscious field of study needs to be developed in America because "it is getting harder to run a Constitution than to frame one . . ." [20]. And why the classic administrative models embodied in the Pendleton Act (civil service reform) and the act to regulate commerce (ICC) emerged in the mid-1880s to bridle the impersonal forces of the "spoilsmen" and "trusts" [21]. And why Secretary of War Elihu Root, who saw firsthand our tragic debacle in the Spanish–American War, instituted a professional general staff concept for the U.S. Army, the very model of classical Hamiltonianism.

In industry, by the 1880s, where the traditional authority of plant managers was breaking down due to the increasing size of the operations, technical complexities, and the demands of expanded national markets, the *routines* and *uniformities* imposed by Frederick Taylor's "scientific management" not only were appealing but critically important. Taylor's mechanistic ideas of *universal laws*, the *one best way*, and the dual deities *economy* and *efficiency* were clear code words that salved the unconscious yearnings of those in quest of unity, purpose, and order in the workplace. The shop was no longer a personal, familiar community but rather a strange, impersonal factory in which the stopwatch, instead of "old Joe," provided the "new order." Taylorism spilled over into government much for the same reasons, though through different routes.

The chief conduit into government for scientific management was New York City's Bureau for Municipal Research, a privately funded, nonprofit research center which between 1900 and 1920 became the "creative center" for Public Administration thinking in the United States. In New York the strains and stresses on the social fabric were most severe as tidal waves of immigrants landed on Ellis Island, taxing neighborhood municipal services to the breaking point.

The New York Bureau of Municipal Research housed a remarkable, dogged group of Public Administration advocates clustered around Frank Goodnow, Henry Bruere, William Allen, Frederick Cleveland, Charles Beard, William Mosher, and Luther Gulick. Many of these men came from social service backgrounds, yet most were academics, and all—to a greater or lesser degree—were imbued with the Christian "social gospel" of bringing "heaven to earth." After seeing firsthand the ineffective and chaotic social services in New York, as Jane Dahlberg has detailed in her excellent book *The New York Bureau of Municipal Research* [22], they dedicated themselves to experimentation with this or that technique and arrived at ad hoc yet strikingly classical Hamiltonian solutions for coping with governmental problems: the centralization of authority in a single individual rather than dispersed in boards or committees, the need for administrative power to be commensurate with responsibility, the importance of a professionalized public service and tenure in office, and the requisites of sound executive tools of budgeting, personnel, organization, and management. Much of what we now know about the fields of budgeting, personnel, organization, and management evolved from the research and discoveries at the Bureau, beginning with their work in 1907 at the New York City Health Department. The Bureau's Training School, begun in 1911, set a standard for excellence in professional training for the public sector unequaled by most universities even today. World War I accelerated this advance in professional training, national centralization, and management technique. By the 1920s many of these ad hoc practical discoveries at the Bureau became solidified into principles of good administrative practice.

Although the two decades between the world wars have been aptly termed by Dwight Waldo the *era of orthodoxy*, the era was "orthodox" only in the sense that theorists *sought* a synthesis of Hamiltonian classicism expressed as scientific principles; they never, in fact, *arrived* at a consensus on precisely what those principles were. Intense debates, which now seem like trivial exercises in medieval scholasticism, raged between the proponents of a *narrow span* of control and the advocates of a *large span*, those who favored *strict separation* of politics and administration and those who favored *lax separation*, those who believed in scientific principles of administration and those who did not, and those who favored appointed executives and those who advocated elected ones. One may laugh at the righteousness and stridency of those debates of yesteryear, but for men and women who were engaged in the practice of public administration at that time, these issues were serious because the stakes were of the utmost seriousness: namely, the very survival of their neighborhood, city, and nation.

The two decades between the World Wars also saw the creative center of public administration shift from New York to Chicago. One of the foremost spokesmen for the field in that period was a shy, introverted political science professor at the University of Chicago, Leonard D. White. White holds the distinction of writing the first public administration textbook in America, *Introduction to the Study of Public Administration* [23], which eventually went into four editions and was hailed as the definitive introductory text in the field. White had a unique stylistic gift (in a field noted for conspicuously turgid prose), an ability to synthesize what was even at that time a vast body of literature and a persistent determination to remain in the forefront, pioneering the "art and science" of Public Administration throughout his academic career at the University of Chicago. Even more fundamental to White's intellectual dominance in this era was the constancy of his philosophical orientation. White pursued his work in the field with a resolute, fixed philosophical compass pointed at classical Hamiltonianism. Some [24] have called his orientation POSDCORB (planning, organizing, staffing, directing, coordinating, reporting, and budgeting). However, on a deeper level his beliefs more accurately reflected a traditional, yet sophisticated development of classicism. This classical orientation is best evidenced by the four assumptions of his text that White outlines in the preface to *Introduction to the Study of Public Administration:* First, he assumes that there is an "essential unity in the process of administration" (or read: there *should* be an essential unity to administrative processes); second, "The study of administration *should* start from a base of management rather than the foundation of law" (or read: emphasis *should* be placed upon activist leadership rather than restrictive rules); third, "Administration is still primarily an art but attaches importance to the significant tendency to transform it into a science" (or read: while public administration primarily involves human relationships, increasingly our focus *should* be directed toward a search for uniformity, routines, and methods to cope with unending social change); and fourth, "Administration is the heart of the problem of modern government" (or read: the real issue in government *should* involve effective design, implementation, and execution of programs, not merely passing new legislation) [25].

The second text in the field, W. F. Willoughby's *The Principles of Public*

Administration [26], published a year after White's, failed to attain the popularity of White's book. Willoughby evidenced a less polished, some- what mechanical prose style, but a more basic problem was Willoughby's emphasis on a legislative dominated administration (shades of Jefferson- ianism?). In short, Willoughby veered too far from the classical Hamilton- ian spirit of that age—an age that looked to Hamiltonianism as the "true," honest, and correct way, *The Way*, to respond to the twentieth century's newly imposed and ongoing crisis of authority.

In 1930, with support from a "trinity" comprising Charles Merriam, chairman of the Political Science Department at the University of Chica- go, Beardsley Ruml, director of the Spelman Fund of the Rockefeller Foun- dation, and Louis Brownlow, former president of the International City Management Association, a flood of Rockefeller monies created an um- brella organization, the Public Administration Clearing House (PACH). Located near the University of Chicago campus, PACH brought together nine diverse public professional associations to share, collect, analyze, and disseminate public sector expertise throughout the United States—the first nationwide consulting firm in the public sector. PACH's identification as a clearing house or simply its second street address "1313" was probably de- vised to encourage informal cooperation—or, in the words of Barry Karl, a sort of "antiorganization"—among its highly individualistic members. PACH, under the astute guidance of Brownlow, became the most power- ful voice of classical Hamiltonianism during the 1930s, reaching its apogee of influence in 1937 with the Report of the President's Committee on Ad- ministrative Management (the Brownlow Report), which was the first officially sanctioned reappraisal of the presidency since 1789. Once again, classical Hamiltonianism was revived in response to a crisis.

This particular institutional crisis was due in large part to Franklin D. Roosevelt's ad hoc approach in responding to the problems of the Depres- sion. Within his first term a vast, sprawling, complex array of administra- tive agencies had been created—all reporting directly to the White House. Even for a canny president like FDR things were getting out of hand. At the end of his first term, presidential authority was severely eroded and poor- ly equipped to deal with the Depression at home and the gathering clouds of an international crisis abroad. Rapid institutional fragmentation coupled with confused lines of authority meant, as the Brownlow Report put it, "the President needs help." In compelling, articulate prose, the Brownlow Report, more than any other public document before or since, summar- ized the essence of three decades of "rebirth" of the classical Hamiltonian administrative pattern [27]:

1. Expand the White House staff so that the President may have a sufficient group of able assistants in own office . . .
2. Strengthen and develop the managerial agencies of the government, particularly those dealing with the budget and efficiency research, with personnel and with planning . . .
3. Extend the merit system, upward, outward, and downward to cover practically all non-policy determining posts; reorganize the civil service system as a part of management under a single, responsible administrator, and create a citizen board to serve as the watchdog of the merit system . . .
4. Overhaul the 100 independent agencies . . . and place them by executive order within one or more of the following 12 major departments . . . and place upon the Executive continuing responsibility for the maintenance of effective organization . . .
5. Establish accountability of the Executive to the Congress by providing a genuine independent postaudit of all fiscal transactions by an auditor-general, and restore to the Executive complete responsibility for accounts and current transactions.

When President Roosevelt read this document, he said, "This is terrific" and changed only one word. By this enthusiastic acceptance, Democrat FDR, who had epitomized romantic Jeffersonianism, embraced classical Hamiltonianism. Rhetoric for many years afterwards, even yet today, has hid this critical shift in orientation. The Brookings criticism notwithstanding, did the president in reality have any alternative? Certainly no president, before and after, would dare campaign on such a platform, though the realities of exercising modern presidential power leave incumbents few options other than stoutly embracing classicism.

The Neoclassical Madisonian Revival in the Post-World War II Era: The Growth and New Authority of the University-Sponsored Empirical Research in the Postindustrial Society

Frequently, Arthur F. Bentley's *The Process of Government* [28] is cited as the "roots of modern political science behavioralism," but, in actuality, his book was little noticed or praised in political science circles at the time of its initial publication; only *after* World War II was it "rediscovered" (the same was true for Max Weber as well). Credit for the renewed emphasis on interest group politics in pre-World War II America rightly belongs to the University of Chicago's Political Science Department. The Chicago School, under the vigorous leadership of Charles Merriam and imbued with the twentieth-century spirit of scientific realism applied to social problems, sought to shift the study of politics from the pre-World War I emphasis on prescriptive, legalistic, and institutional methodology to the new analytical, empirical realism, termed *behavior science*. What emerged from the "revolt" at the Chicago School, beginning in the 1920s, was an impressive body of literature which endeavored to show the policy process "as it really was"—the product of a complex interplay of interest groups. The following books were characteristic of this behavioral analysis: Peter Odegard, *Pressure Politics, The Story of the Anti-Saloon League* [29]; Stuart Rice, *Farmers and Workers in American Politics* [30]; Elmer E. Schattschneider, *Politics, Pressures and the Tariff* [31]; and E. Pendleton Herring, *Group Representation Before Congress* [32] and *Public Administration and the Public Interest* [33].

In the same years, Elton Mayo and his associates at the Harvard Business School, after a decade of intensive empirical research at Western Electric Company in Chicago, were discovering the "great illumination"—namely, that informal groups (or read: *interest groups*) inside formal organizations had more to do with the productivity of a firm than the rational application of "outside" scientific management techniques. Likewise, Chester Barnard's *The Functions of the Executive* [34], as well as the psychologically insightful writings of Mary Parker Follett, espoused a "new view" of executive decision making in organizations derived from pluralistic rather than monolithic power. These works, however, were only preludes to the explosive "reawakening" of the neoclassical Madisonian spirit in postwar America.

The Depression and World War II brought academics into government in droves. This firsthand exposure to the realities of public administration with all its complexities left many with the lasting impression that this was "where the action was." More specifically, the view from the inside looked dramatically different from the classical theories of Goodnow's, White's, and Gulick's "principles." Moreover, the waves of European intellectuals who had fled the specter of Nazism—men such as Carl Friedrich, Fritz Morstein-Marx, and Alfred Diament—enriched the American study of bureaucracy by introducing broader European attitudes and perspectives into American political science. These immigrants were impressed by the sheer enormity and power of America both domestically and internationally. Their contributions to the literature are studded with an intense, though sophisticated, nationalism—an enthusiasm for American democracy—which is often characteristic of first-generation Americans.

Furthermore, the lives of millions of Americans in the postwar era were directly touched for the first time by the activities of public administrators staffing an expanded bureaucracy on the local, state, national, and international scene. Social Security checks, draft notices, FHA/VA mortgages, and the emergence of the nuclear age made public administration worthy of everyone's serious attention. Civilization now hung precariously on what a myriad of unknown public administrators did or did not do.

Moreover, rapid expansion of American universities and colleges amply endowed with public funding gave a new postwar stimulus to intensive research into public administration. Members in scholarly organizations such as the American Political Science Association increased from 1300 in 1920 to 3000 in 1945 to 15,800 in 1972. New specialized organizations and journals such as the American Society for Public Administration and its house journal, *Public Administration Review*, emerged to provide outlets for scholarship, dialogue, and discussion about public administration.

Among the descriptions of the postwar America were Daniel Bell's "postindustrial society," Don Price's "scientific estate," Zbigniew Brzezinski's the "technetronic era," and Frederick C. Mosher's the "professional state." Whatever epitaph was applied to the epoch of postwar America, the fount of new knowledge and authority flowed from the intellectual base housed within university and research centers across the nation and was supported generously by public and private grants. In Daniel Bell's view, "if the dominant figures of the past hundred years have been the entrepreneur, the businessman, and the industrial executive, the 'new men' are the scientists, the mathematicians, the economists, and the engineers of the new computer technology" [35]. The postwar rise of the university with its empirical and scientific outlook drastically altered the thrust of Public Administration as a field of study. The pre-World War II public administration fraternity had been dominated by men like Merriam, Gulick, and Brownlow, who were part-time academics and part-time practitioners/consultants—men concerned about practical government. They had forged an action-oriented, prescriptive study of administration that reflected their intense involvement as "insiders." Postwar administrative theorists were to a large extent dominated by academics whose writings expressed a considerably more process-oriented, analytical, detached, and descriptive perspective—in short, a neoclassical Madisonian outlook.

The first wave of renewal in Madisonian realism hit the old pre-World War II classical Hamiltonians like a bombshell. To the older public administration "hands," it seemed not only as if their world had been turned upside down but as if the very purpose for the study was now called into question. In his classic *The Administrative State* [36], Dwight Waldo examined Public Administration prior to World War II through a long-range telescope of the "great western philosophical questions"—e.g., who should rule, what is the good life, etc. —and pointed out the fundamental ambiguities, ironies, and problems inherent in classical orthodoxy. Waldo placed classicism squarely within the context of the great traditions of political theory. Certainly, this was "shocking," yet his view offered wider and more profound perspectives about the field. Herbert Simon's *Administrative Behavior* [37], on the other hand, placed Public Administration theory under the high-powered microscope of logical positivism. Simon equally jolted the public administration fraternity of that period not only by finding contradictions in the older classical "proverbs" of administration but by seeking resourcefully, though unsuccessfully, to rebuild the entire field on a groundwork of a new, yet shaky, fact–value dichotomy. From the vantage point of a seasoned New Deal practitioner turned Maxwell School dean, Paul Appleby attacked the old, pious, prewar platitudes of administration, preaching a new pluralism with his prolific pen, beginning with *Big Democracy* [38]. So devastating were these attacks on the old dogmas that by 1949 Yale Professor James W. Fesler wondered, in print, if nothing that had been learned about administration in the last generation was still usable.

Certainly, Public Administration had learned something. In fact, it had "learned," or more accurately "relearned," quite a lot about classicism, and now postwar scholars were relearning another "old administrative tradition," neoclassicism. The Madisonian weltanschauung was, however, strikingly different from Hamiltonianism: it was based on dispassionate empirical analysis of human behavior "as it is," not "as it should be," and focused on the complex interplay of interest groups involved in the formation of public policy. By the 1950s many schools of neoclassical Madisonian scholarship had emerged in America (in many ways more alike than their "followers" realized): first, the *politics-in-administration school,* based on writings of Paul Appleby, Norton Long, and others, who stressed how multiple interests inside and outside of government significantly shape administrative decisions; second, the *decision-making school,* disciples of Herbert Simon, who emphasized interdisciplinary analysis of the "decision" as the main event in public administration; third, the *case method,* through the efforts of Harold Stein and others, which focused on the pluralistic nature of public policy making by objective and careful description of particular administrative episodes (cases); fourth, the *human relation school,* building on the prewar work of the Hawthorne experiments and the postwar writings of Bennis, McGregor, Likert, Argyris, Maslow, and others, who examined the influence of multiple informal interest groups in large-scale formal organizations; fifth and sixth, the broader *organization theory* and *comparative administration schools*, represented by the scholarship of Bertram Gross, Fred Riggs, Ferrel Heady, and Robert Dahl, who echoed broader pluralistic perspectives through systems theory and cross-cultural analysis [39].

It was Yale economist Charles Lindblom, however, who best synthesized the neoclassical Madisonian spirit of the age as applied to Public Administration in his brief but popular essay "The Science of Muddling Through" (reprinted, up to now, over 40 times in various textbooks) [40]. Here, the public administrator was no longer a "doer" governed by "principles" or separated from politics in a unified administration system as White had envisioned. Nor was he, in Lindblom's terms, the "optimal rationalizer" of "efficiency and effectiveness." Rather, the public administrator practiced the "art of the possible" in a complex, pluralistic world of competitive interest groups. Public Administration became less like chess and more like poker. Negotiation and strategy were the tools of an administrator's trade, aimed chiefly toward producing an "agreeable" compromise. He "muddled," not "managed." Yet this difficult, confused act of incremental decision making, argued Lindblom (in the true neoclassical Madisonian spirit), was in the best interest of society. It produced social harmony, stability, unity, and equilibrium in a fluid, unstable environment of an ever-changing sea of interest groups. Here was a revival of Madisonian neoclassicism stated in its most clear, concise, comprehensive format. Yale, not Chicago, was now the creative focal point of Public Administration (although at the time, ironically, Yale was viewed as being "hostile" to the field).

However persuasive Lindblom and others may have been for the Madisonian perspective, by and large, they did not destroy or significantly alter enthusiasm in some quarters for Hamiltonian classicism; they only supplemented it. Ironically, many of the same professors who by day propounded clear-eyed neoclassicism in the classroom would by night fly to Washington where they would turn into hot-blooded advocates of Hamiltonian classicism. Hamiltonian classicism did indeed thrive in this era, but primarily it did so near or inside the corridors of power where the chief dilemmas turned on questions of not who rules but rather how to survive. One only needs to read the first Hoover Commission Report (1949)—aptly called "Mr. Brownlow's children" by Herman Finer—to discover how Madisonian academics turned into Hamiltonians when they grappled with the practical use of governmental power. On the local level as well, Madisonian academics became ardent Hamiltonian advocates for either strong mayor or city manager forms of government [41].

Nevertheless, the intense debates within Public Administration circles were *not* between the Madisonian-versus-Hamiltonian views (which were frequently advocated by the same person) but rather between "various schools of pluralism," particularly over the "purity" of this or that particular behavioral methodology. In retrospect, these arguments—many of which continue even today—seem not only monotonous but quaint as well. As Dwight Waldo aptly observed of these controversies [42]:

> Behavioralists, like Marxists and Protestant Christians, have sometimes presented a more or less unified front against the "enemy"; but—like Marxists and Protestant Christians—they have often disputed and contested among themselves—over doctrine, strategy, tactics, and objectives.

Public Administration Thought since Minnowbrook: A Democratic Surge and the Revival of Romantic Jeffersonianism

The late 1960s and early 1970s witnessed, in the words of Samuel P. Huntington, a "democratic surge" characteristic of past historic eras of Jeffersonian-Jacksonian democracy and progressive reform where there was a vital reassertion in all phases of American life of democratic idealism. As Huntington argues, the era reflected [43]:

> general challenge to the existing system of authority, public and private. In one form or another, this challenge manifested itself in the family, the university, business, public and private associations, politics, the governmental bureaucracy and the military service. People no longer felt the same compulsion to obey those whom they had previously considered superior to themselves in age, rank, status, expertise, character or talents. Within most organizations, discipline eased and differences in status became blurred. Each group claimed its right to participate equally—and perhaps more equally in the decision making which affected itself. More precisely, in American society, authority had been commonly based on: organizational position, economic wealth, specialized expertise, legal competence, or electorial representation. Authority based on hierarchy, expertise and wealth all obviously ran counter to the democratic and equalitarian temper of the times.

While the reasons for the sudden democratic surge were complex and are, even now, still unclear, Huntington points to a number of significant *consequences* of the democratic surge [43]:

1. Expansion in the size and scope of governmental activity, though with a concomitant decline in governmental authority;

2. Increased public interest and concern about government, but coupled with a sharp decline in public trust and confidence toward government;

3. Increased public activism in politics, yet with a commensurate decay in the traditional two-party system;

4. A noticeable shift away from coalitions supporting government to those in opposition to it.

Characteristic of this period was a popular philosophical treatise by John Rawls, *A Theory of Justice* [44], that defined justice in largely egalitarian terms. In the fields of history and politics, Arthur Schlesinger's *Imperial Presidency* [45] found an enthusiastic post-Watergate audience with an argument directed against the flagrant abuses of strong executive institutions in American government. Also, egalitarian themes found their way into economics, particularly in E. F. Schumacher's *Small Is Beautiful* [46], which proposed a more equitable distribution of the goods and services in society directed toward, in the words of its subtitle, *As If People Mattered*.

At the same time a similar emphasis on equity thrived in the literature of Public Administration; it began with a group of "younger" academics in *Toward a New Public Administration, The Minnowbrook Perspective* (1971), edited by Frank Marini [47]. Bored with the dry realism of the postwar behavioralists, in search of new intellectual foundations for Public Administration, caught up in the egalitarian enthusiasms of the moment, and concerned with the "excessive abuses" of bureaucratic authority in Vietnam and elsewhere, the *New Public Administrationists* wanted to make a fresh beginning for the field. Although the essays contained in the *The Minnowbrook Perspective* seem loosely linked with one another, even at times contradictory, there was evidence of common themes of participation, consensus, decentralization, trust, and even love of mankind. However, the essence of their weltanschauung was perhaps best captured in two words of one author, H. George Frederickson: *social equity* [48]. Although few of the proponents of the New Public Administration realized it, paradoxically, their "new message" harkened back to the very old roots of nineteenth-century romantic Jeffersonianism. Were the New Public Administration revolutionaries really "new" or throwbacks to yesteryear?

Another popular and controversial Public Administration scholarly treatise in the 1970s was Vincent Ostrom's *The Intellectual Crisis in American Public Administration* [49]. In his book Ostrom frontally assaults the "classical Hamiltonian model," which he terms the *Wilson–Weber paradigm*. In behavioral language reminiscent of Herbert Simon a generation earlier, Ostrom proposes its replacement with a new paradigm, one which he calls *democratic administration*. Ostrom's book generated unprecedented scholarly debate on the whole range of its contents, starting with its philosophic premise regarding whether or not Public Administration roots did indeed rest on Wilson–Weber's writings.

In reality, though, Ostrom's democratic administration paradigm attracted popular interest *because of* its forceful emphasis on *democratizing* administration. Ostrom argued *against* "single-centered administrative power," "hierarchical administration," and "separation of politics from administration" and *for* "diverse democratic decision making centers," "popular participation in administration," and "dispersed administrative authority based upon structures of overlapping jurisdiction and fragmented organizations." Jeffersonian enthusiasm for the village values of grass roots democracy, the New England town meeting, even surreptitiously crept into his thesis by means of Ostrom's wholesale advocacy of Buchanan, Tullock, Olson, and Niskanen's models of political economy, whereby every citizen gets to vote with his feet or pocketbooks on virtually all public services at the grass roots. Under the murky guise of political economy, Ostrom hid a lusty enthusiasm for that old-time religion of romantic Jeffersonianism.

Although the 1970s saw a strong resurgence of older romantic Jeffersonian themes, classical and neoclassical models thrived as well. Particularly, the closer one moved to the "dilemmas of governance," the more intensely classicism blossomed. A staggering array of new alphabetized schemes were tried in the 1960s and 1970s from PPBS (planning-programming-budgeting system), to MBO (management-by-objectives), to ZBB (zero-based budgeting) to bring coherence, unity, efficiency, and effectiveness to an increasingly weak and fragmented government at all levels —ghosts of Hamiltonian classicism?

Neoclassical Madisonian perspectives also found an equal number of adherents during the same period. The rich veins of interest group writings continued unabated from the pens of scholars (many from Yale) such as Wildavasky, Lindblom, Kaufman, Simon, Thompson, Golembiewski, and Schick, who reached out to a wide, enthusiastic college audience. Even though Dwight Waldo and others saw public administration beginning with the late 1960s in an "era of identity crisis," by the early 1980s, as issues of energy, inflation, military preparedness, economic scarcity, institutional cutbacks, and international instability became more insistent, the participatory themes of a decade earlier were clearly "fading" in influence and popularity. The field in the early 1980s could almost be characterized in much the same way as the 1880s and 1780s where familiar classical models waxed as urgent crises demanding effective national authority became apparent at home or abroad. The wheel turns, sometimes in reverse.

Conclusion: Public Administration in a Nation without a Crown

At the outset, we asked whether Public Administration could find a place in the new American nation, a nation "without a crown." The absence of the stable moorings of a feudal tradition, as Gordon Wood, Louis Hartz, and others have pointed out, gave America a distinctly monotonous political ideology; it also gave America a maddeningly elusive administrative theory. Like a schizophrenic personality, American Public Administration has projected over its history a "triple persona," reflecting and affecting the hidden flux of national political authority. Nineteenth-century Public Administration theory and practice appeared in the guise of romantic Jeffersonianism, mirroring weak public institutions framed in the lost personal world of island communities. The 1880s and 1890s saw a dramatic fragmentation of village society and a new centralization of American institutional authority. The "redressing" of Public Administration in the forms of classical Hamiltonianism came as a vital response to the sudden collapse of the old social order. Here, classicism was more than a mere idea; it flourished as a vital weapon used in the fight for community survival.

The reappearance of the "cooler" perspectives of neoclassical Madisonianism after World War II paralleled the rise of a new postindustrial state forged on the imperatives of empirical analysis and scientific research generated in universities, government, and business. Neoclassicism, however, supplemented, not supplanted, classicism. The democratic surge in the late 1960s and early 1970s brought simultaneously increased popular participation in politics and a sudden decline in the institutional authority of government. A new burst of enthusiasm for romantic Jeffersonian administrative perspectives emerged momentarily in the same period as the twin contradictory tendencies of popularism and institutional decay.

Although a single administrative identity may have dominated each era, none has done so at the total exclusion of the others. Traces of Hamiltonianism can be uncovered throughout the nineteenth century, just as Jeffersonianism or Madisonianism crops up here and there, sometimes intensely, in the early twentieth century. Nevertheless, the dominant patterns of Public Administration thought that can be viewed in major American historic epochs have been clearly influenced by the complex ebb and flow of public authority. Considerable blending and merging and many shades of gray can be found among administrative patterns, so that, in fact, there have been relatively few "pure moments" of classicism, romanticism, or neoclassicism.

No doubt it is the peculiar maleable nature of American Public Administration, due in large part to our own complex changing structure of national authority, that makes the field so difficult, if not impossible, to export abroad to other cultures. No doubt, also, the same perplexing, idiosyncratic elusiveness of the field accounts for the intense, periodic "generational revolts" that have rocked the field over the course of its history. Even within the same generation, practitioner "insiders" who are intimately involved with the dilemmas of government and who frequently embrace, out of necessity, classicist perspectives find they cannot communicate in the same language with romantic- or neoclassical-inclined "academics" who may be more "objectively" detached from the responsibilities of governing. They talk at or pass each other and wonder how the others can*not* understand. Public Administration, to these and many others, may seem a strange, confused, and even exasperating amalgam that defies a common, coherent definition—though it also remains an exciting, worthwhile, and even "noble" intellectual pursuit concerned with, to borrow a phrase of Carl Friedrich, the very "core of modern government."

Acknowledgments

The author is indebted to the following individuals who thoughtfully read and criticized a draft version of this chapter: Frederick C. Mosher, Ferrel Heady, Brack Brown, Harold Gortner, and Laurence J. O'Toole, Jr.

References

1. Gordon Wood, *The Creation of the American Republic 1776–87*, University of North Carolina Press, Chapel Hill, 1969.
2. Leonard D. White, *The Federalists: A Study in Administrative History*, Macmillan, New York, 1948, p. 478.
3. "The Continentalist, No. 1, July 12, 1781," in *The Papers of Alexander Hamilton*, vol. II, Columbia University Press, New York, 1964, p. 651.
4. Clinton Rossiter, *Alexander Hamilton and the Constitution*, Harcourt Brace, New York, 1964, p. 162.
5. Wilson Cary McWilliams, *The Idea of Fraternity in America*, University of California Press, Berkeley, Calif., 1973, pp. 209–210.

6. "Jefferson to James Madison," December 20, 1787, in *The Writings of Thomas Jefferson*, vol. VI, Thomas Jefferson Memorial Foundation, Washington, D.C., 1903–1905, pp. 392–393.
7. "Jefferson to Samuel Kercheval," July 12, 1816, in *The Writings of Thomas Jefferson*, vol. XV, Thomas Jefferson Memorial Foundation, Washington, D.C., 1903–1905, p. 33. On the whole, Jeffersonian political philosophy was considerably more complex *in practice* than his pronouncements suggest. While he extolled the virtues of popular sovereignty, legislative supremacy, and limited executive authority, Jefferson as president certainly stretched executive powers in his conduct of an undeclared war against the Barbary Coast Pirates, in his lack of fiscal authorization for the purchase of the Louisiana Territory by Congress until *after the fact*, and in his enthusiastic endorsement of such public works projects as roads, canals, and schools.
8. Lynton K. Caldwell, *The Administrative Theories of Hamilton and Jefferson: Their Contribution to Thought on Public Administration*, University of Chicago Press, Chicago, 1944, pp. 236–241.
9. James Madison, "The Federalist, No. 10," in Edmund M. Earle (ed.), *The Federalist*, Random House, New York, 1937, p. 54.
10. "To Thomas Jefferson," October 24, 1787, in *The Writings of Thomas Jefferson*, vol. IX, Thomas Jefferson Memorial Foundation, Washington, D.C., 1903–1905, pp. 523–524. It is worth underscoring here that while Madison did recognize the diversity of interests in society as a source of conflict, he found that the root cause of problems "has been the various and unequal distribution of property" (*Federalist 10*).
11. Samuel P. Huntington, "The Founding Fathers and the Division of Powers," in Arthur Maass (ed.), *Area and Power*, Free Press, New York, 1959, p. 183.
12. James Madison, "The Federalist, No. 51," In Edmund M. Earle (ed.), *The Federalist*, Random House, New York, 1937, p. 337.
13. Ralph Ketcham, *James Madison: A Biography*, Macmillan, New York, 1971, p. 301.
14. Leonard D. White, *The Jacksonians*, Macmillan, New York, 1954, p. 46.
15. Herbert Kaufman, "Emerging Conflicts in the Doctrines of Public Administration," *The American Political Science Review*, 50 (December 1956):1057–1073. However, it should be emphasized that the "democratizing" of the public service came gradually rather than abruptly as Sidney H. Aronson's analysis confirms. His statistical comparison of the appointments of John Adams, Jefferson, and Jackson to the top federal service positions shows only a slight change in broader repre-

sentation of diverse interests in America. See Sidney H. Aronson, *Status and Kinship in the Higher Civil Service,* Harvard University Press, Cambridge, Mass., 1964.

16. Robert H. Wiebe, *The Search for Order, 1877–1920,* Hill & Wang, New York, 1967, pp. xiii–xiv.

17. Alexis de Tocqueville, *Democracy in America,* vol. I, Knopf, New York, 1945, pp. 95–96, 219.

18. Douglas Southall Freeman, *Lee's Lieutenants: A Study in Command,* 3 vols., Scribner, New York, 1942–1944.

19. Matthew Crensen, *The Federal Machine,* Johns Hopkins University Press, Baltimore, 1975.

20. Woodrow Wilson, "The Study of Administration," *Political Science Quarterly,* June 1887, pp. 197–222.

21. Perhaps by linking *impersonal* with the term *boss* I may confuse and mislead some readers because it is common for modern political scientists and sociologists to point out the "humanizing" roles which nineteenth-century political machine leaders played, particularly with respect to new European immigrants to American cities. However, my point is that in the minds of many American reformers at the turn of the century the term *boss* was a remote, impersonal, even fearful force worthy of total eradication.

22. Jane Dahlberg, *The New York Bureau of Municipal Research,* New York University Press, New York, 1966.

23. Leonard D. White, *Introduction to the Study of Public Administration,* Macmillan, New York, 1926.

24. Dwight Waldo, *Perspectives on Administration,* University of Alabama Press, University, Ala., 1956. It should be noted that the term *POSDCORB* was actually coined more than a decade *after* the appearance of the first edition of White's textbook. Waldo argues, however, that White adopted essentially a POSDCORB perspective, meaning that White and Luther Gulick's outlooks and philosophies regarding the field had considerable similarity to one another.

25. Leonard D. White, *Introduction to the Study of Public Administration,* Macmillan, New York, 1926, pp. vii–viii.

26. W. F. Willoughby, *The Principles of Public Administration,* Johns Hopkins University Press, Baltimore, 1927.

27. "Report of the President's Committee on Administrative Management," in Frederick C. Mosher (ed.), *Basic Documents of American Public Administration, 1776–1950,* Holmes & Meier, New York, 1976, pp. 135–136.

28. Arthur F. Bentley, *The Processes of Government*, Macmillan, New York, 1907.
29. Peter H. Odegard, *Pressure Politics: The Story of the Anti-Saloon League*, Columbia University Press, New York, 1928.
30. Stuart Rice, *Farmers and Workers in American Politics*, Columbia University Press, New York, 1924.
31. Elmer E. Schattschneider, *Politics, Pressures and the Tariff*, Prentice Hall, New York, 1935.
32. E. Pendleton Herring, *Group Representation Before Congress*, Russell & Russell, New York, 1929.
33. E. Pendleton Herring, *Public Administration and the Public Interest*, McGraw-Hill, New York, 1936.
34. Chester Barnard, *The Functions of the Executive*, Harvard University Press, Cambridge, Mass., 1938.
35. Daniel Bell, "Notes on the Post-Industrial Society," *The Public Interest*, 6 (Winter 1967):24–35; Zbigniew Brzezinski, *Between Two Ages: America's Role in the Technetronic Era*, Viking, New York, 1970; Don K. Price, *The Scientific Estate*, Harvard University Press, Cambridge, Mass., 1965; and Frederick C. Mosher, *Democracy and the Public Service*, Oxford University Press, New York, 1968.
36. Dwight Waldo, *The Administrative State*, Ronald Press, New York, 1948.
37. Herbert Simon, *Administrative Behavior*, Macmillan, New York, 1945.
38. Paul Appleby, *Big Democracy*, Alfred A. Knopf, New York, 1945.
39. In preparing this section on postwar Public Administration, I am indebeted to Frederick C. Mosher (ed.), *American Public Administration: Past, Present, Future*, University of Alabama Press, University, Ala., 1975.
40. Charles E. Lindblom, "The Science of Muddling Through," *Public Administration Review*, 19 (Spring 1959):79–88.
41. For example, see the arguments of a well-known pluralist scholar for strengthening large city managerial capacities in Wallace S. Sayre, "The General Manager Idea for Large Cities," *Public Administration Review*, 14 (Autumn 1954):253–258.
42. Dwight Waldo, "Political Science: Tradition, Discipline, Profession, Science, Enterprise," in Fred I. Greenstein and Nelson W. Polsby (eds.), *Handbook of Political Science: Scope and Theory*, vol. I, Addison-Wesley, Reading, Mass., 1975, pp. 59–60.
43. Samuel P. Huntington, "The United States," in Michael Crozier (ed.),

The Crisis of Democracy, New York University Press, New York, 1975, pp. 74–75.

44. John Rawls, *A Theory of Justice*, Harvard University Press, Cambridge, Mass., 1971.

45. Arthur Schlesinger, *Imperial Presidency*, Houghton Mifflin, Boston, 1973.

46. E. F. Schumacher, *Small Is Beautiful: Economics As If People Mattered*, Harper & Row, New York, 1973.

47. Frank Marini (ed.), *Toward a New Public Administration: The Minnowbrook Perspective*, Chandler, Scranton, Pa., 1971.

48. George H. Frederickson, "Toward a New Public Administration," in Frank Marini (ed.), *Toward a New Public Administration: The Minnowbrook Perspective*, Chandler, Scranton, Pa., 1971, p. 311. For an excellent commentary on the New Public Administration, read Laurence J. O'Toole, Jr., "Lineage, Continuity, Frederickson, and the 'New Public Administration,' " *Administration and Society*, 9 (August 1977):223–253.

49. Vincent Ostrom, *The Intellectual Crisis in American Public Administration*, 1st, 2nd eds., University of Alabama Press, University, Ala., 1973, 1974. It should be noted that while the New Public Administration movement and Ostrom's writings belong to the same historic period and share many of the same ideas of Jeffersonian romanticism (especially in their opposition to classical administrative ideas), they derive their origins, followers, and methodological foundations from distinctly different sources. In other words, they both would no doubt agree on what they dislike, but as with connoisseurs of fine wines, there would be ample dispute over what constitutes the "very best."

2

The Theory and Practice of Public Administration as a Science of the Artifactual

Vincent Ostrom
Indiana University, Bloomington, Indiana

Organization is viewed as an artifact that embodies consideration of both factual elements and value elements. Values are potentially knowable through intersubjective comparisons mediated by reference to language. Human organizations are a form of word-ordered relationships that rely heavily upon value terms and the structuring of rules, rulers, and ruled. Two models of such relationships are developed with reference to a theory of sovereignty and a theory of constitutional rule. Public service economies can be organized with reference to varying institutional arrangements. Production functions require recourse to forms of knowledge appropriate to the type of service being supplied. Thus the craft of public administration opens to a universality of knowledge, skills, and interests not confined to a single discipline.

Introduction

The behavioral tradition in the social sciences proceeded on an assumption that the methods of the natural sciences were appropriate to the study of social phenomena. From this perspective it was the function of scholarship to develop the basic knowledge of uniformities that applied to social phenomena. Once the basic laws of social relationships were known, then they could be applied by practitioners, such as those concerned with the practice of public administration.

If we begin, however, with a presumption that social phenomena are essentially artifactual in nature, we have a somewhat different problem in conceptualizing the relationships inherent in the theory and practice of public administration. Administration is then viewed as a work of art or as an artifact. An artifact is anything created by human beings by using learning and knowledge to serve human purposes. The task and process involved in the creation of an artifact will be referred to as artisanship.

The relation of an artisan to the creation of an artifact implies that both instrumental knowledge and considerations of value are built into the basic nature of an artifact. Artisanship always requires the use of certain materials that are then transformed into an artifact. This transformation requires the use of instrumental knowledge that is appropriate to the techniques for producing an artifact. The use of basic knowledge becomes an integral part of all artisanship.

But any artisan also draws upon conceptions about the purpose to be served by an artifact and a sense of proportion about what constitutes a good artifact. These considerations are built into an artifact just as much as the material ingredients that are used. But the two different types of "ingredients" are not simply mixed together. Rather the basic conceptions held, the sense of proportion, and the criteria of choice serve as imaginary templets that enable an artisan to construct, shape, or fashion an artifact. An artifact can be both a practical utensil and a thing of beauty. Both are built into the nature of an artifact. One value need not detract from the other.

All artifacts thus represent a union of *factual* elements and *valuational* elements. It is not possible to have a value-free artifact. A theory of artisanship requires reference to the place of values that serve as criteria to guide the choices an artisan makes both in selecting materials and in the purposes and meaning that are articulated in an artifact.

The craft of public administration involves a complex pattern of relationship between artisans and their creations. If we view organization to be a fundamental tool in the craft of administration, we need to first recognize that organizations are subject to design and creation like any other artifact. Those who use a tool need not be the same ones who designed and created a tool. Yet any artisan needs to know the logic that is inherent in a tool if he or she is to be aware of both its potentialities and its limitations.

Artisans who use organizations as tools are also the primary ingredients of organizations. Organizations, in effect, are artifacts that contain their own artisans. Those who form an organization are also engaged in some form of joint artisanship in which a collective effort is made to produce some service or effect that can be viewed as an artifact.

In exploring the theory and practice of public administration as a science of the artifactual, I shall first turn to the problem of values. I shall then consider the basic problem of authority relationships inherent in all organizations and examine two different models of authority relationships that apply to the organization of human societies. These models will then be extended to apply to the organization of two different types of administrative systems for organizing a public service economy. Finally, consideration will be given to the organization of production functions applicable to the particular types of service agencies. In conclusion, I shall indicate how a science of the artifactual requires recourse to multiple levels of meaning.

The Problem of Value

In exploring the problem of value I shall rely predominantly upon the analysis made by Thomas Hobbes in *Leviathan*. There Hobbes indicates that once an array of alternative possibilities is available, all human choice is based on two different types of calculations. The first set of calculations is to determine the probable consequences to be associated with each alternative. The second set of calculations is to weigh those alternatives with reference to one's preferences and aversions. A choice is made of that alternative that offers the best prospect of advancing one's potential well-being. Whatever is the object of a desire or an appetite can be initially defined as good and the object of an aversion as evil. The nature of good or evil is not intrinsic to objects themselves but is derived from human nature.

In social relationships where individuals are required to take into account the interests of others, Hobbes suggests that we cannot know what preferences and aversions others will have for particular objects. But underlying these preferences and aversions for particular objects is a "similitude of thoughts and passions" that is characteristic of all mankind. From this similitude of thoughts and passions, any one person can come to understand the way others think and feel. By first learning to read oneself, one can learn to read others. Those characteristics that are common to mankind are the universal characteristics of human nature.

If those who govern can read in themselves all mankind, Hobbes reasons that law can then provide the appropriate measure of right and wrong, justice and injustice, lawful and unlawful. But we need not be limited to this conclusion. If each individual has the potential of reading oneself and coming to understand others, each should be able to arrive at basic standards of right and wrong that meet with the concurrence of others. A common standard of value would enable each individual to act in relation to others as one would have others act in relation to oneself. With a common standard of right and wrong, individuals could make decisions that take into account each other's essential well-being. A limited ground thus exists for making intersubjective comparisons of basic value considerations. Such limited grounds can be supplemented by providing others with opportunities to articulate their own perceptions and preferences.

The extent to which human beings share a common source of intelligibility reflected in a similitude of thoughts and passions should enable them to develop common measures of value for distinguishing right from wrong, the just from the unjust, the true from the false, and the beautiful from the ugly. But such measures of value depend on a shared community of understanding developed by those who are willing to inquire into the nature of their own being as that which is shared in common with other beings. It is from sharing a common source of intelligibility that human beings have the prospect of participating in an artisanship where each can share an understanding of what others do, take into preliminary account the interests of others, and provide others with opportunities to communicate their interests and preferences.

A neglect of fundamental values derived from a common source of intelligibility can lead human beings to create organizational artifacts that destroy their own artisans. Such possibilities easily arise from the nature of authority relationships. Yet they are hardly congruent with the fuller realization of human intelligibility. To explore this problem, we need to consider the basic structure of authority relationships.

The Basic Structure of Authority Relationships

All patterns of human social organization depend on the use of words for ordering interpersonal relationships. Words are used to formulate rules that facilitate some forms of conduct and constrain others. The basis for partitioning conduct into that which is lawful and unlawful is derived from value criteria inherent in moral precepts. Rules, presumably, are derived to rig or structure the game of life in ways that will be mutually productive or mutually beneficial to those who participate in organized endeavors.

The difficulty arises from the circumstance that rules are artifacts created as a matter of human choice. People can act both in conformity to rules and at variance with rules. Short-term expedience may deviate from long-term interest, and immediate self-interest may vary from one's self-interest that has taken into account the interests of others. Incentives may exist for individuals to act at variance with rules. The question then is how to make rules binding in human relationships.

The method used in most human societies is to rely upon the agency of some individuals to exercise special prerogatives that have to do with the enforcement of rules. This implies that allocation of authority to some who will function as rulers to maintain and enforce rules in relation to others. These are the prerogatives associated with the processes of governance in all social relationships: Rules imply rulers and ruled.

The prerogatives of rule involve the capacity to impose sanctions or penalties upon those who fail to act in accordance with the requirements of rules. The imposition of sanctions or penalties is adverse to the interests of those who are subject to their impositions and thus is in the nature of an evil. Those who exercise the prerogatives of rule are lawfully vested with authority to use instruments of evil to enforce rules and gain the advantage of rule-ordered relationships. All organization thus depends on a Faustian bargain in which instruments of evil are used as necessary means to realize some common or joint good.

The availability of such instruments of evil creates an opportunity for those who have access to their legitimate use to exploit others and dominate the allocation of values in a society. Organization is then transformed into a situation in which the few can exploit the many. The instruments of evil come to dominate human social relationships, and the potential of mutually beneficial relationships erodes into one of exploitation, resistance, and repression.

Rule-ordered relationships are the source of most fundamental inequalities in human societies. Increases in the degree of equality under law are usually accompanied by increasing inequalities between those who exercise the prerogatives of rule and those who are subject to their rule.

The relationship among rulers, rules, and ruled can easily be transformed into a situation in which organizations become artifacts that destroy their own artisans. The iron law of oligarchy prevails, and the few dominate and exploit the many. Whether or not these patterns prevail depends, in part, on the way that basic authority relationships are organized in human societies. Two broadly different models have been formulated for the organization of such relationships.

One model relies upon a unitary structure of authority relationships in which coordination is attained through a common system of law that derives from having a single, ultimate center of authority as the common source of law. This model is perhaps best articulated in Hobbes's theory of sovereignty. In Hobbes's solution, some one person or some one body of persons must be vested with the ultimate authority of government and have the last say in making the basic decisions in any society. Since such a center of authority is the source of law, it is above the law and cannot itself be held accountable to law. The authority of those who exercise sovereign prerogatives is unlimited and indivisible. Inequality between rulers and ruled assumes absolute proportions. The peace and concord of subjects derives from their obedience to authority. Hobbes sees no other way that human beings can gain the benefits of organized society without the existence of some single center of ultimate authority to assure the coordination of a structure of rule-ordered relationships. His theory of sovereignty is probably the most widely used model of authority relationships in the world today.

Another model, perhaps most fully articulated in the American efforts to develop a system of constitutional rule and explained in *The Federalist Papers,* is based on a presumption that rules for the organization and conduct of government can be specified as fundamental law. With an appropriate structure, enforceable limts of constitutional law can then be maintained with reference to those who exercise governmental prerogatives. Such a possibility depends on the development of a structure of relationships that forecloses dominance by any one center of authority and places limits upon all exercises of authority.

The organizational requisites for such a system of government are a complex allocation and distribution of authority relationships. In the American theory of constitutional rule, fundamental law is distinguished from ordinary law, and processes of constitutional decision making are distinguished from governmental decision making. Governments are not free to alter fundamental law. The rules that bind governments are instead subject to the more general constitutional authority exercised by the people. Ordinary laws, however, can be enacted and modified by governmental authorities.

The terms of a constitution itself, in turn, typically distribute authority in a complex way. First, the basic authority of persons and citizens is delineated as inalienable rights that in turn represent limits on the authority of government in general. Further, the authority of government is distributed among diverse decision structures so that each will have an independent role in formulating law, determining its application, and enforcing law. Concurrence among the diverse decision structures is required for collective action. The veto positions available to each decision structure imply limits to the authority of other decision structures. The political feasibility of any one form of collective action then depends on the pursuit of possibilities within the conceptual space provided by the respective veto positions for the different decision structures. Such a structure can maintain an equilibrium within the constraints of the respective veto positions without having recourse to a single, ultimate center of authority [1]. A polycentric order can thus be maintained where all exercise of governmental authority is bounded by the rules of constitutional law rather than having recourse to an ultimate center of authority that is above the law [2].

These constitutional constraints can be further reinforced by provisions for either the direct or indirect participation of citizens within the processes of government. Methods of voting and representation allow for indirect participation. Reliance on juries and grand juries in judicial processes involves direct citizen participation in decisions taken by courts. In the case of grand juries that have jurisdiction to inquire into the discharge of public trusts, citizens have an opportunity to participate directly in inquiries pertaining to the performance of public officials more generally.

Principles of constitutional rule can be significantly amplified through the organization of concurrent governments representing overlapping communities of interest. Each government can be bound by limits inherent in fundamental law: All governments are subject to law, and no unit of government is above the law. Diverse legal, political, administrative, and constitutional remedies can be sought through different units of government. No one government is allowed to exercise a monopoly over the legitimate use of force in society organized on the basis of federalism and constitutional rule.

A system of enforceable constitutional rule is based on a presumption that people in such a society can draw upon a common body of understanding reflected in a common theory of constitutional choice, commonly accepted moral precepts, and metaphysical presuppositions. So long as such understandings are shared in common and citizens take decisions that are consistent with the maintenance of limits in the organization and conduct of government, we can consider democracies to be a viable form of government in the sense that people can be said to rule: "demo" = *people;* "cracy" = *rule.* If such limits are abandoned, a democracy ceases to exist and gives way to the iron law of oligarchy where the few rule the many.

In considering problems of organizational analysis and design, it is essential that students and practitioners of public administration take the perspective of constitutional choice and consider all those factors that might lead to a choice among alternative organizational possibilities. This is especially important in a democratic society where the basic viability of such a society depends on the maintenance of essential limits in the creation of all organizational arrangements. Considerations of basic metaphysical presuppositions and moral precepts, and the places that these have in the common understanding and agreement about the basic terms and conditions of government, presumably are applicable to all different levels of organization in a democratic society. A knowledge about the capabilities and limitations of different types of institutional arrangements is also relevant to the level of analysis that would inform constitutional choice.

Since constitutional choice is defined as that level of choice that applies to the rules pertaining to the organization and conduct of government, all levels of decision making that apply to subordinate structures of government are appropriately viewed by artisans as constitutional choice. This may apply to legislators considering legislation that would serve as a "charter" for an agency, to executive officials formulating reorganization plans, to courts mandating constitutional remedies that alter the structure of organizational relationships, or to intergovernmental contracts specifying joint-operating responsibilities. A contract can be used to constitute new forms of enduring relationships. The potential for using the perspective of constitutional choice can be explored by considering alternative principles that might be applied to the organization of a public service economy.

Organization of a Public Service Economy

Students and practitioners of public administration have relied predominantly upon a theory of bureaucracy as the basis for conceptualizing relationships within and among public agencies. Concepts such as unity of command, span of control, and hierarchical ordering of authority relationships have been those used in aggregating structures of agency and interagency relationships in the public sector. Coordination is presumably attained by having recourse to one single source of executive authority as expressed in the concept of unity of command.

When viewed from the perspective of constitutional choice and applied to interagency relationships as well as intra-agency relationships, the principles associated with bureaucratic organization are consonant with Hobbes's theory of sovereignty and do not allow for the distribution of authority that is consistent with a democratic theory of constitutional rule. Tocqueville, who was thoroughly familiar with the French system of bureaucratic administration, recognized in *Democracy in America* that the American system of public administration operated on principles substantially at variance with French bureaucracy. The American system of decentralized administration involved a multitude of relatively independent functionaries who were constrained more by electoral controls and judicial controls than control by administrative superiors. Yet Tocqueville saw a system that was surprisingly robust with the provision of roads, schools, and other public services that compared favorably to those found in Europe.

The traditional theory of administration contained a fundamental principle—span of control—that implied limitations on hierarchically ordered relationships. This principle held that each supervisor had only limited capabilities for deriving information and exercising control over subordinates. Only a small number of subordinates could be effectively monitored by any one supervisor. Some have assumed that the maintenance of a narrow span of control provided a management principle which would surmount this difficulty. Herbert Simon, however, pointed out that loss of information and control will occur in the number of levels of supervisory control as well as in the span of control applied at any one supervisory level [3]. The effort to solve the problem by a narrow span of control is frustrated by the loss of information and control with more levels of organization.

More recently, Gordon Tullock has articulated a general theory of bureaucracy in which he expects bureaucratic structures to filter information in a way that creates systematic distortions and biases in information and generates serious problems of institutional weakness and failure [4]. From a perspective of constitutional choice, serious problems of institutional failure and weakness would suggest that a search for alternative ways of organizing administrative structures is in order.

Contemporary work on the theory of public goods suggests that the essential difficulties requiring recourse to governmental organizations occur on the consumption side of economic relationships [5]. The failure of exclusion and jointness of use as the two criteria pertaining to the nature of public goods and services poses difficulties that require collective organization of consumption functions so as to foreclose holdouts, coerce payments in the form of taxes, articulate and aggregate demands, make decisions about the appropriate levels of service, and monitor the levels of service provided. Once these consumption functions are organized collectively, production of the appropriate type and level of service can be arranged through alternative sources of supply. Contractual arrangements between units of government serving as collective-consumption units and private vendors or other governmental units can be used to arrange the supply of a service as well as supplying services through their own staffs.

Under these circumstances, quasi-market conditions can exist between production and consumption units in a public service economy. If competitive pressures are maintained and fiscal arrangements are appropriately monitored, there is reason to believe that such quasi-market arrangements can enhance efficiency by more closely proportioning supply to variability in demand and in capturing diverse economies-of-scale in organizing both the production and consumption functions in a public economy. These possibilities are entirely congruent with the administrative system that Tocqueville characterized in *Democracy in America*.

Since both theory and practice enable us to contemplate alternatively structured systems of administration, a constitutional choice perspective would suggest that each alternative be carefully assessed for its capabilities and limitations. When theoretical analysis leads to contradictory conclusions, empirical research would be warranted where the performance characteristics of different systems can be compared under similar circumstances.

These conceptions in turn need to be considered in the context of a more general system of authority relationships. The requirements for the creation and maintenance of a democratic society, in particular, imply substantial constraints on the range of choices that may be available. Unity of command implies a monocentric order, and a monocentric order takes us to Hobbes's theory of sovereignty. The requirements of a democracy depend on foreclosing that option and attempting to create a polycentric order in which all exercise of authority is constrained by enforceable rules of law.

In the modern preoccupation with professionalism, students and practitioners of public administration are apt to neglect the place that persons and citizens have in the performance of an administrative system. Persons and citizens may, indeed, be important coproducers of essential public services. Teachers, for example, cannot produce education without the active collaboration of students. Nor can police produce peace and security without the active collaboration of members of a community. Too frequently the design of bureaucratic, organizational arrangements gives little attention to how professionals and those whom they serve can develop the best collaborative arrangements for pursuing their joint interests.

Whenever the boundaries of administrative relationships are drawn so as to exclude those who are being served and to deny them an effective voice in organizing collaborative efforts, administrators are likely to neglect essential interests.

Since collective endeavors are presumably organized so that human beings can be of mutual help to one another, the perspective of constitutional choice would also suggest that those who analyze and design organizational arrangements take the perspectives of others and allow others to speak for themselves in articulating their essential interests. Unless collective efforts are of mutual benefit, they simply become instruments for some to exploit others. The most grievous error that can be made is for analysts to take the perspective of the omniscient observer and to presume that they can, like God, take into full account all interests.

Conceptualizing the appropriate nature of organizational relations reflects the conditions that apply to the joint artisanship that is to be undertaken in any collective effort. Those concerned with the craft of administration need also to consider the conceptualization and design of the basic product or service that is the object of their artisanship. This requires access to still a different universe of inquiry.

Production Functions

The service activities of administrative agencies are always concerned with some desired result or product to be realized. These vary significantly from service to service. The artisanship inherent in producing a service requires attention to the materials used and the transformation necessary to yield the desired effect. The calculations inherent in the performance of any production function require an instrumental knowledge that draws upon the appropriate scientific traditions. But the use of that knowledge is also directed to some range of effects that reflect human preferences and thus the proportioning of conditions is being directed to yield the *desired* effects. Both instrumental knowledge and considerations of value are being taken into account in the organization of production functions.

The organization of different production functions requires access to quite different forms of knowledge and the use of different forms of technology. Production functions in water resource administration, for example, are fundamentally different from those associated with educational administration. In the one case the preoccupation is primarily concerned with hydraulic characteristics of water as a liquid and the way that human beings can either take advantage of different characteristics of water or reduce the damage that might otherwise accrue from those flow character-istics. Various types of engineering provide the appropriate bodies of knowledge pertaining to different uses of water and are reflected in the generation of hydroelectric energy, fish and wild life management, remov-al and discharge of wastes, regulation of flows for flood control purposes, navigation, and the diversion and use of water for irrigation, domestic, and industrial purposes.

In the case of education, the transformation that is occurring is with ref-erence to changes in students as human subjects. The change is with refer-ence to the development of knowledge and skills associated with learning. But the transmission of learning among human beings requires access to those who already possess the appropriate knowledge and skills acquired from prior learning. As education advances to more specialized bodies of learning, the field of educational administration requires cognizance of the whole universe of learning. The term *university* indicates the universality of interests that preoccupy the educational enterprise at higher levels of learning.

The craft of public administration, like universities as collective en-deavors, opens out to a universality of knowledge, skills, and interests. Rather than being a discipline in the sense of being preoccupied with a par-ticular type of knowledge, public administration requires artisans who are grounded in all different fields of knowledge. Such a diversity of knowl-edge does not foreclose the possibility of diverse artisans sharing in a methodology of artisanship where a common appreciation for the require-ments of artisanship lays the foundation for collaboration among many different types of artisans. The methodology of artisanship, like the methodology of scholarship, can be organized to facilitate the mutual en-lightenment of those who participate in the process.

Many of the specialized fields of administration draw upon closely re-lated bodies of knowledge and technological processes that facilitate strong communities of interest among participants. The recurrent nature of the problems confronting those who participate in the fields of water resource administration, health services, educational services, welfare services, fire protection, police protection, collective security, and other closely related services means that they share a community of interests where coordination is easily attained among artisans who know what needs to be done in confronting problems of mutual interests. If we view similarities in shared knowledge and production technologies as applying to particular crafts, we would expect similar craftsmen to be brought to-gether in the performance of similar production functions to produce particular types of services. All would share a community of interest derived from the nature of the craft, and agency boundaries need not be serious impediments to collaborative efforts so long as mutual advantage could be derived from collaborative efforts.

Communities of professional interests tend to cluster with reference to types of service. In such circumstances we might look upon interagency arrangements as a collaborative milieu that brings like artisans together in the practice of their craft. Opportunities for various forms of voluntary association among persons engaged in the crafts of public administration can occur in the context of these shared communities of interest that transcend particular agency relationships.

Conclusion

A science of the artifactual has reference to many different levels of meaning. Even in the case of the simplest artifact, explanations require reference to the materials, knowledge, and technologies used in producing an artifact. These, in turn, need to be supplemented by an understanding of the purposes served. Considerations of utility and beauty may both be embodied in an artifact. Both *facts* and *values* are built into artifacts, and it makes no sense to speak of a value-free artifact or value-free artisanship.

When extended to a study of organizations as artifacts, complex levels of meaning need to be taken into account. Organizations as artifacts include their own artisans. The initial design of an organization is based on instrumental knowledge of how conditions can be expected to yield consequences. Both the range of alternatives that are considered to be available and the criteria of choice pertaining to the purposes to be served become essential elements of meaning in fashioning an organization. These considerations must then be translated into prescriptive rules for ordering relationships among the individuals involved. The very words used in rule-ordered relationships involve value terms relative to rights, duties, wrongs, remedies, etc. These are the value-impregnated means that, in turn, are being used to realize the purposes of joint benefit to larger communities of people. The very question of deciding what boundaries are to apply in defining the domain of organizations is likely to be a highly arbitrary one, which determines what orders of meaning are to be taken into account in thinking about organizations.

Whatever orders of meaning are encompassed within an organization, we need to recognize that those who are included are themselves artisans who use existing decision structures as tools for relating themselves to others. They, too, need to know the logic that is inherent in the tool if they are to make effective use of it. But tools may be used in ways that are different from those intended by their designers. Thus, the way that tools are used may have quite diferent meanings in varying circumstances, as those who refer to goal displacement in bureaucracies have recognized.

A science of the artifactual thus requires reference to many different levels of meaning when we recognize the role of artisans in the creation of artifacts and when we recognize that organizations as artifacts contain their own artisans. An appropriate logic of inquiry requires that the method of the natural sciences be supplemented with an interpretive or hermeneutical approach to clarify the way that the different levels of meaning are shaped into a coherent structure of meaning [6]. If that general structure of meaning can then be used to specify the logic of a situation, the approach of rational choice theory might be used to derive inferences about how representative individuals, or other units of analysis, would act in such situations. By applying these methods to different levels of analysis [7], we might hope to develop a science of the artifactual that would be appropriate to the study and practice of public administration.

Such a science should also make us more sensitive to some of the basic moral problems involved. All organizations represent Faustian bargains that require potential recourse to evil to do good. The use of evil to do good is the basic ingredient for tragedies unless used with extraordinary precautions.

Acknowledgments

I wish to acknowledge the generous support of the workshop staff in the preparation of this manuscript and of Indiana University in the support of my research efforts.

References

1. W. Ross Ashby, *Design for a Brain*, rev. ed., Wiley, New York, 1960. Here Ashby develops a veto theorem (p. 79) and its implication in the ultrastable system (pp. 80–99).
2. Michael Polanyi, *The Logic of Liberty*, University of Chicago Press, Chicago, 1951. Polanyi first developed the concept of polycentricity.
3. Herbert A. Simon, *Administrative Behavior*, Free Press, New York, 1965.

4. Gordon Tullock, *The Politics of Bureaucracy*, Public Affairs Press, Washington, D.C., 1965.
5. Vincent Ostrom and Elinor Ostrom, "Public Goods and Public Choices," in E. S. Savas (ed.), *Alternatives for Delivering Public Services*, Westview Press, Boulder, 1977.
6. J. Donald Moon, "The Logic of Political Inquiry: A Synthesis of Opposed Perspectives," in Fred I. Greenstein and Nelson Polsby (eds.), *Political Science: Scope and Inquiry*, Addison-Wesley, Reading, Mass., 1975, pp. 131–228, especially pp. 154–206. Moon's discussion of an interpretative or hermeneutical approach, together with a rational choice approach, would appear to offer the best promise for a science of the artifactual.
7. Phillip M Gregg, "Units and Levels of Analysis: A Problem of Policy Analysis in Federal Systems," *Publius*, IV (1974):59–86.

3

Toward Democracy within and through Administration: A Primer to Inspire and Guide OD Applications

Robert T. Golembiewski
University of Georgia, Athens, Georgia, and
University of Calgary, Calgary, Alberta, Canada

In this chapter the author seeks to contribute to the reconceptualization of the basic task of administrative theory in public administration. The standard approach—here called democracy versus administration—pairs the will of governance inspired by a republican spirit with an autocratically guided work of governance. In short, the bureaucratic principles seek to put autocracy in the service of republican democracy.

Three major points are made about this momentous pairing. Substantial research supports the conclusion that bureaucratic organization implies major individual and organizational costs. In addition, evidence suggests that this approach to organizing impacts negatively on attitudes and behaviors that seem appropriate for citizens of republics. Finally, details are provided about how Organization Development (OD) suggests an evolving alternative to the bureaucratic model—an alternative whose values are more democratic than autocratic and whose constituent designs often have positive effects on efficiency and effectiveness. In sum, OD theory and designs are not seen as a panacea for what ails bureaucracy. But that theory and those designs have two major virtues: They permit energizing multiple forms of democracy, with special effect in small- to moderate-sized aggregates, and they permit building useful attitudinal and behavioral supports for OD values that contrast sharply with the normative fundamentals of bureaucratic principles.

The purpose of this chapter is to highlight a central irony or paradox within public administration theory. Mainstream conceptual approaches to public administration over the past half-century or so have sought to put organizational autocracy in the service of democracy. Such approaches have been characterized elsewhere in terms of the opposition *democracy versus administration* [1]. The opposition means that the work of governance is organized in terms of bureaucratic principles, even as the will of governance is motivated by a republican spirit. Redford calls this a "simple model of overhead democracy" and further asserts that [2]

> democratic control should run through a single line from the representatives of the people to all those who exercised power in the name of government. The line ran from the people to their representatives in the Presidency and the Congress, and from there to the President as chief executive, then to departments, then to bureaus, then to lesser units, and so on to the fingertips of administration. Exceptions to the single line were acceptable only for the judiciary, and perhaps also for certain quasi-judicial and quasi-legislative functions and the auditing function.

Although Redford believes that *overhead democracy* is an effective means to protect democratic values while operating within a bureaucratic setting, he also considers this model too simplistic. It does not adequately describe administration as it operates, nor does it prescribe how efficient or effective administration should be.

Robert Dahl adds to this discussion by identifying several more or less "democratic" levels for forming the political will, ranging from primary democracy to polyarchy, which he links to the administration of government by the overhead democracy model. But, paradoxically, he notes [3]

> you will need administration, and administration will need hierarchy. Otherwise the people who rule may turn out to be *not* the people but the bureaucrats. I do not see how we can stretch the meaning of democratic authority to include the hierarchy of administration. Consequently . . . rule by the people requires not only democratic forms, but also non-democratic forms of delegated authority.

In this chapter we shall seek to clarify the apparent irony or paradox inherent in the democracy-versus-administration model by moving toward the development of models for democracy *in* administration and democracy *through* administration. Three major points are developed. First, continued use of the democracy-versus-administration model implies major individual and organizational costs which can no longer be justified. Second, emerging evidence suggests that organizational autocracy tends to corrode the bases of republican government, even as it is intended to save and serve it. And third, Organization Development (OD) will be shown to provide reasonable alternatives to the bureaucratic model for organizing work which are more consistent with our republican political heritage and which can contribute to organizational efficiency and effectiveness.

Bureaucracy Impacts Individuals and Organizations

Within the framework of the democracy-versus-administration model, one might note a *traditional structure* approach (see Figure 1) and a *flow of work structure* approach (see Figure 2). By reviewing each of the approaches under three points of analysis, the significant liabilities which Model I (Figure 1) presents to the existence of democratic values in bureaucratic settings become apparent. This discussion will focus on each model's implications for individuals and for organizations within a public sector environment.

In brief introduction, Model I has a family of characteristics that can

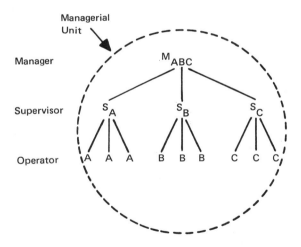

Figure 1 Traditional structure. *Model I.* A structure consistent with values of bureaucracy: emphasis on differentiation, repression, stability, and function. Underlying properties: Authority is a vertical, or hierarchical, relation. Departments are organized around the same or similar activities, called *functions* at high levels of organization and *processes* at low levels. That is, "like" activities are put together. Only a relatively small number of people should report directly to any superior. (From Ref. 4, Part 2, p. 38.)

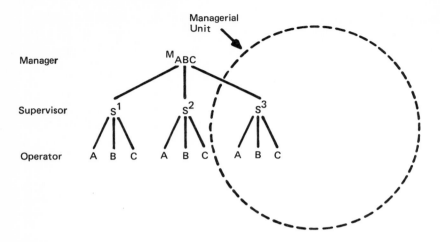

Figure 2 Flow of work structure. *Model II.* An alternative structure: emphasis on integration, self-control, change, and flow of work. Underlying properties: Authoritative relations occur up, down, and across the organization, and all these vectors should support shared goals. Departmentation reflects the flow of work; that is, related activities are put together whether they are "like" or "unlike." A relatively large number of people may report to any superior, given a structure that facilitates measuring performance. (From Ref. 4, Part 2, p. 39.)

have serious dysfunctions under a broad range of conditions. For example, Model I structures require a large *managerial unit*, defined as that portion of an organization monitored by some authority in a position to make reasonable decisions about a total flow of work. Only M_{ABC} is in such a position in Model I, and M_{ABC} typically will energize specific processes and styles in order to function in that structure. Hence centralization will tend to prevail; long communication chains must be developed to link levels of recognition, decision, and implementation; work will tend to be fragmented so as to enhance top-level control; and supervisory styles will tend toward the autocratic or directive. These conditions are typically associated with low satisfaction and often with low productivity.

Model II (Figure 2) suggests an alternative structure which adapts easily to decentralization, project management, independent profit centers, management by objectives, autonomous teams, job enrichment, and numerous other variations. This unorthodox model groups together all or most activities required for a total flow of work. By departmentalizing around related activities, whether they are "like" or "unlike," this model permits each supervisor to control a managerial unit, and this leads to profound consequences such as shortening the distance between decision and action and encouraging identification with a whole flow of work rather than a particularistic contribution. In addition, Model II seeks minimum control consistent with end-item quality and quantity. The multiple opportunities for self-discipline and self-control built into the model, for example, reduce the need for overhead efforts for direct and detailed control. Teams, whose performance is easily and meaningfully comparable, control the flow of work.

Some Implications for Individuals

Many ways could be chosen to develop the implications of the two alternative models for individual behavior and attitudes. Model I jeopardizes employees' identification with and ownership of work. Most recently, its influences have been seen in reference to people at the lower levels of organization where the incidence and virulence of "blue-collar blues" abound [5]. At higher levels of organization, the awkward effects of Model I structures were first highlighted in the radical reorganization efforts undertaken by several industrial and commercial giants a half-century ago. Similar counterproductive influences have more recently been noted in the public sector in such agencies as NASA [6].

Model I structures reinforce this loss of identification with and ownership of work in a variety of ways. The common insistence on democracy versus administration forces reliance on a narrow range of means for influencing behavior that often has a high "pain-to-gain" ratio. Kelman distinguishes three behavior-influencing modes or processes [7]:

Compliance, in which case the influence is accepted to receive some reward or avoid some punishment controlled by the influencing agent
Identification, in which case the influence is accepted so as to maintain or develop a satisfying relationship with the influencing agent
Internalization, in which case the influence is accepted because it is congruent with the learner's own value system

Thus bureaucracy emphasizes the compliance mode, which carries with it very mixed virtues. Bureaucracy often complicates, if it does not preclude, individual needs for internalization. The traditional structure is so need-depriving that it encourages psychological avoidance, if not rejection, of work. In combination these factors reduce organizational effectiveness, especially in the sense that internalization implies the greatest potential for self-starting and self-controlling behaviors, the kinds of behaviors that not only simplify organizational life but also energize it.

Some Implications for Organizations

The contrasts between Models I and II may imply a *contingency view* which suggests that the kind of effective organizational structure will vary with the conditions, internal and external, which the organization faces. Possible contingent conditions cover a wide range. Four polarities are suggested as illustrative. Depending on the emphasis placed on one pole or the other of these four continua, different structures will be appropriate.

Differentiation → Integration Today's organizational needs often require a movement from differentiation toward integration, a thrust which basically derives from product complexity, numerous required specialties, and shortened time frames. Managers must develop strategies which promote motivation and collaboration regardless of the existing organizational structure. In Model I structures, each department provides only a partial contribution to a variety of flows of work, and this increases the level of difficulty in factoring out success or failure. Hence, fragmentation under Model I organizations must be guarded against.

In contrast, Model II structures require that managers perform a motivating and collaborating role in situations which permit decentralized patterns of delegation to promote a climate of trust and reduce fear, conformity, and dependence. Thus, integration becomes a preeminent objective [8]. Shared values which supersede prevailing bureaucratic values must be developed and broadly accepted regardless of structural change. Obtaining acceptance of these values in principle—free and open communication, sufficient emotional as well as rational/technical expression, and acceptance of constructive conflict—and working toward them in practice constitute major challenges.

Influence Repression → Influence Enhancement Historically, under the Model I approach, people were fitted to meet the organization's needs. More recent approaches, such as Model II, urge the shaping of organizations to fit people. As it has become more clear that the needs of individuals are frustrated in Model I organizations, management has begun to recognize and deal with the problems of individual and group repression and influence in organizations.

In the public sector two basic approaches to structural change to facilitate individual influence have been taken. First, Model II structures assist in alleviating the problems of individual influence in the organization by encouraging self-discipline and self-control. Such developments provide greater opportunities for individuals to measure performance more accurately. Second, and more commonly, reliance has been placed in various counterbalances to the traditional structuring of work. Examples include the use of team building to improve interpersonal relationships and the development of new forms of organizational due process and influence sharing. Such changes are often difficult to implement.

Stability → Planned Change Whether one proposes that "smaller is better" or that "onward and upward" still suffices, it appears that organizational life requires a growing emphasis on planned change. Any such shift implies at least two major challenges as one compares Model I and Model II. First, the change function must be given priority, with attendant policies and procedures which better equip people to tolerate ambiguity and dislocation. Given Model I's tendency toward stability and certainty, basic questions remain as to how to successfully move in this direction. Some clues to such a process exist, but we are far from having adequate knowledge in this area.

Second, an emphasis on planned change implies a growing need to develop and disband both large and small work units quickly as today's organizations adapt to tomorrow's projects. More or less temporary systems require that people develop a kind of instant but still intense commitment and learn to cope with the loss of temporary systems in ways which do not inhibit their commitment to future systems. Only recently have theory and experience in this area been gathered (see Ref. 4, Part 2, pp. 185–214).

Function → Flow of Work The shift from function to flow of work allows organizations to respond more effectively to contemporary challenges, but not without costs. Model I structures tend to be less supportive of the flow of work emphasis than Model II structures, particularly in the critical area of employee involvement. The Model II structure generates a bottom-up approach to organizing work, and while that facilitates the measurement and motivation of performance, it also severely tests the skills of managers. For example, effective Model II managers tend to approach risk and trust in ways not encouraged by Model I structures. The latter structures are rooted in mistrust as reflected in narrow spans of control and a bias toward directive or autocratic supervisory styles.

In addition, Model II structures imply the need to manage multiple references and identifications. Consider the implied reorientation in staff personnel from a dominant, centralized identification with "management" to a strong identification with specific work units. This requires that staff personnel resist "giving away the store" and also that they provide continuing support for overhead interests and policies. Model I structures finesse these difficult emotional and political issues by emphasizing central identification and control.

Consequences of Bureaucratic Structure in Public Loci

A shift to a public sector focus suggests three prominent features for consideration. Adherence to the bureaucratic model (Model I) is a persistent and pervasive characteristic of public sector organizations because of the dominance there of the perceived conflict between democratic and administrative values and practices [9]. As compared to the private sector where marked efforts to break away from bureaucratic constraints permeate recent theory and practice, the bureaucratic model and its influences appear to be more nagging and advanced in the public sector, with only rare stirrings of theory and practice dealing with attendant problems. Illustratively, Rourke and Peabody's 1965 review of diverse areas of organizational research still applies; for example [10],

"Generalizations about organization morale, job satisfaction and productivity . . . have largely been based on research undertaken in industrial firms."
Concerning the "broad area of research [dealing] with organizational structure . . . , many of the studies have taken place outside of public bureaucracies."
In decision making, the "models have largely been based on price determination and other problems of industrial firms" (see Ref. 11, pp. 807, 810, 813, 816).

Another approach suggests that negative features of the bureaucratic model impact with special force in the public sector where the model is reinforced by civil service systems which have as their goal the safeguarding of governmental administration from the influences of partisan politics. The apparent lack of evidence available in this regard is noted by Rainey [12] in a study which provides some intriguing comparisons of middle-level managers in public sector and business organizations. With appropriate reservations, he reports data relevant to an oft-asserted serious problem among public personnel: the harmful influence of civil service systems on incentives and motivation. He notes that middle-level public managers report weaker connections between performance and personal incentives, that they score lower on several facets of work satisfaction, and that formal personnel procedures constrain them in their ability to recognize and reward superior performance.

Several caveats appear to be in order. The available research can hardly be considered conclusive, although several studies point toward similar observations [11,13,14]. Moreover, some (but not many) observers seriously question whether the differences noted above apply generally [15]. Furthermore, available studies do not necessarily indicate that government managers are lower in motivation or performance, all other things being more or less equal. Indeed, given differences in the kind of work, compensation packages, and job security among others, that demonstration would be difficult to make without additional directed research.

Bureaucracy Undercuts Democratic Ideals

Not only are individuals and organizations impacted by the bureaucratic environment, but democracy versus administration undercuts the basic democratic values which it purports to protect. Klein has phrased this position well [16]:

> the manner in which employees participate in work life of their companies is critical for the use they make of formal mechanisms for representation and consultation and also for their attitudes of constructive interest, of satisfaction, and of dissatisfaction. [The] bulk of scientific evidence suggests that the more the individual is enabled to exercise control over his task and to relate his efforts to those of his fellows the more likely he is to accept a positive commitment. The positive commitment shows that personal initiative and creativity which constitutes the basis of democratic climate [which has relevance not only to work but extends far beyond it].

Although it is readily acknowledged that life experiences impact on political performance [17], few studies seek to explore the influence of work-site experiences on political behavior and preferences. Commentators have noted that representative government takes on a variety of forms in Western political cultures. However, authoritarian and sometimes autocratic structures tend to predominate in public and private administrative organizations. Since for most people the work-site experience consumes a significant proportion of daily activity, it appears plausible, if not probable, that such experiences condition individual responses to non-work-related concerns. For this reason it appears necessary to bring work-site experiences and governance into a closer balance. Maccoby suggests improvements in the quality of work life (QWL) based on the following general values [18]:

> *Increased security.* The first area of security involves health and safety, which we intend to improve by creating the best possible environment, with a minimum of hazards. Security against loss of job is

more difficult to achieve. . . . No one can promise that a worker will never be laid off. In the *overall* sense, security from loss of job depends on effectively operating the plant to assure recovering the major portion of the available business, so that the plant continues in business and continues employing workers.

Increased equity. By making the distribution of work, the organization of work, the rewards of work, and the rules under which we work as fair and as reasonable as they can be.

Increased individuation. By recognizing that all people are not the same, but have different interests and needs, and by increasing the opportunities for people to develop in their own ways.

Increased democracy. By giving each worker more opportunities to have a say in the decisions that affect his life, including his work life.

In QWL efforts with values like those listed, democratic forms of political governance do not suffice. The emphasis shifts to creating authority structures *at work* which will permit people to develop resources for participative politics. As Elden notes, this "inverts the popular radical cry" [19].* Drawing further on Elden, this yearning-cum-direction industrial or organizational democracy commonly seeks to avoid some such self-fulfilling cycle [19]:

Ideology and technology emphasize centralized and heirarchical control. ⟷	Jobs are simplified and repetitive; employees are "hands."
↑	↑
"Democratic elitism" evolves, since few have necessary resources to participate effectively.	The "mind-functions"—planning, supervision, and so on—are reserved to higher hierarchical levels.
↑	↑
Employees develop few politically-relevant resources: they are socialized into passivity, they learn powerlessness, accept low political efficacy, and may resort to "compensatory leisure." ⟷	Employees reflect low "educational potential": they are discouraged from seeking higher-level skills as well as from exerting control over their worksite.

*See also J. Maxwell Elden, "Political Efficacy at Work: The Connection Between More Autonomous Forms of Workplace Organization and a More Participatory Politics," *The American Political Science Review,* 75(1) (March 1981):43–58.

Such a cycle, more or less compatible with bureaucracy, poorly suits the requirements of political democracy.

But over the last two decades, alternatives to this common approach to organizing work have been sought with increasing vigor. The incongruence between the expected behaviors of individuals in the political and work arenas has received the attention of an increasing number of researchers. Moreover, a primary impetus for such attention stems from increasing evidence that associates negative motivational and economic outcomes with the traditional approach to organizing work [4]. Included among these negative economic and emotional impacts are low satisfaction, low output, high absenteeism, and generally low motivation.

Aversion to the preceding cycle transcends ideology. Beginning with early work with supervisory styles and group decision making, aspects of an applied organizational science have evolved somewhat unevenly. Several alternatives for organizing work have been developed: job enrichment [20], autonomous teams [21], sociotechnical variants [22], and organizing around flows of work versus functions [23]. They all tend toward a definite ideal type. This alternative ideal type would have properties that, according to Elden, contrast sharply with properties of the bureaucratic model for organizing work [19]:

| | Contrasting authority structures | |
Function	Hierarchical/elitist	Self-managed/ democratic
Basic unit for work organization	One man, one job	A group which aggregates related tasks necessary for a flow of work
Flow of control and relevant information	Basically vertical	Up, down, or across the organization, as the situation requires
Work routines	Fragmented and simplified; little learning possible	Integrated into "whole" tasks with variety, learning possibilities, and intrinsic rewards
Locus for handling	Next highest organizational level above level where variance occurs	Within a group or a team as a whole; little variance is "exported" upward in the hierarchy

These contrasting authority structures coincide nicely with Models I and II respectively.

The alternative model rests on two fundamental tenets. First, it implies that individuals have a kind of internal gyroscope—some set of basic needs or preferences toward which people tend, at least when they have a reasonable opportunity to do so or sometimes even when that opportunity is limited and/or hazardous. In general, the gyroscope is oriented toward the direction of increased competence, comprehensiveness, and growth. Second, the alternative model implies the power of small groups—in meeting individual needs for intimacy, acceptance, and security as well as for setting and maintaining norms that legitimate certain ranges of behavior while proscribing others.

Serious consideration of the alternative model is merited when one notes that the bureaucratic model neglects individual predispositions toward growth and comprehensiveness, especially at lower organizational levels. This need deprivation is frustrating and results in low satisfaction and/or productivity, which seem common abreactions to frustration. In addition, the traditional model tends to neglect groups or to see them as dysfunctional, even seeking to undercut them so as to make individuals more dependent on authority figures. By emphasizing vertical and one-to-one relationships, the traditional model facilitates two probable effects. The formation of groups may be inhibited, and many individuals will suffer need deprivation, resulting in low satisfaction and/or productivity. Alternatively, underground groups may develop and persist, despite the contrary thrust of the traditional model and its underlying philosophy. In such cases groups often will be highly cohesive and possess contramanagement norms. Within such groups satisfaction levels may be high mainly because such groups control their work site and can successfully hassle management. But productivity will tend to remain low.

The key questions concerning the political attitudes and behaviors generated by such alternative approaches to organizing work have seldom been embodied in explicit research designs. However, a few studies provide insights into such efforts. Consider one study [24,25] which raises the following key question: If a work site were set up to reflect the self-managed/democratic alternative for organizing work, would favorable consequences on broader political attitudes and behavior result?

The research focused on three sets of consequences: those affecting the work unit, those impacting on work itself, and those affecting political outcomes beyond the work site. As for the last, relevant questionnaire items focused on:

Personal potency, or the degree as to which one is powerless and controlled by fate or luck;

Political efficacy, which measures one's attitude to being able to influence government and seems to covary with the degree of political participation by individuals;

Social participation, which relates to the degree that individuals involve themselves in various discretionary-time organizations, i.e., those oriented to community, public service, and so on.

The results? Elden identified the following major covariants of the self-managed/democratic alternative for organizing work [19]:

democratized authority structures are likely to benefit individual workers (more work satisfaction, personal development, and skills acquisition); their organization (increased identification and contribution as reflected for example in better quality, less absenteeism and turnover); and their social class or society as a whole (increased political resources more widely diffused and decreased alienation).

In sum, Elden believes that one's willingness to engage in participatory opportunities will covary with the extent to which that person possesses power over his or her work: "Empirically there appears to be a *political dimension to everyday worklife*" [19].

Such conclusions should still be couched in tentative terms, but they encourage additional and urgent interest in this line of research.

Toward Administration that Reinforces Democratic Ideals

Given the two sets of negative effects of the bureaucratic model related to efficiency and effectiveness as well as to political socialization, we propose that through Organization Development (OD) democratic ideals may be reinforced within the administrative setting rather than diminished. We shall focus on the following:

Some reasonable concerns that are inadequately responded to by the bureaucratic model;

Action research, which can be responsive to these reasonable concerns and yet avoids the rigidities of *positivist science,* especially with regard to values;

A global description of Organization Development whose thrust emphasizes its value-loaded character;

Illustrations of how specific OD designs can make administration less co-
ercive and more effective at several levels of complexity.

Bureaucracy's Inadequate Responses to Reasonable Concerns

Several major reasonable concerns underlying democracy versus administration that have been awkwardly responded to will profit from elaboration. First, of most importance, democratic values encourage an active
concern about unchecked administrative power. This concern, which evi-
dently motivates the general acceptance of the bureaucratic model, often
goes too far. It exacerbates the problem of control, rather than simplifying
it. Numerous cases illustrate that bureaucratic controls can stifle and sup-
press the useful flow of information. The concern to follow bucreaucratic
routing often results in an inadequate flow from the determination of
public policy in the political process to the actual implementation of policy
goals and objectives.

In addition, relatively noncoercive regimes cannot persist without relatively widespread popular support. However, popular support is not
guaranteed or perhaps even encouraged by the bureaucratic model,
whether one considers bureaucracy in its "ideal" state or in its actual performance. Moreover, the costs of bureaucracy in terms of effectiveness
and political socialization, as already discussed, seem far more likely to
erode popular support than to enhance it. Last, democracy versus administration proposes to serve broader democratic systemic values through an
organizational arrangement which tends to violate those same values
within its internal structure. That strategy will seldom serve as a useful
long-run strategy, given the propensity to increase the bureaucratic functions when problems grow near overwhelming and when knowledge concerning alternatives tends to be lacking.

Third, the bureaucratic model promotes hierarchy as the basic safeguard against collusion, corruption, or the nurturance of a technological
elite. For the most part, hierarchy is used as a device to enhance upper-
level control over lower-level positions, but could have just the opposite
results.

Appleby addresses this problem by noting that democratic morality derives basically from two sources: from an open and multirepresentational
form of politics, which exposes administration to processes of review and
evaluation, and from hierarchy, but hierarchy seen more as a vehicle for
broadening the perspective applied to a decision than as a command–obey
linkage [26]. From Appleby's perspective, the critical task has two aspects:
It involves maximizing the former sense of hierarchy on the major issues,

and it urges minimizing a sense of hierarchy that dominates. Bureaucratic principles seem to encourage directive or autocratic supervision rather than a more participative decision process.

Last, democracy versus administration and the associated traditional bureaucracy imply that the needs of public employees are not the only or even the primary needs to be served. Conventional wisdom may go so far as to infer that attention to employee needs takes away from the bureau's ability to perform its tasks. Thus any concern regarding employee needs has relevance only insofar as it impacts upon job-related performance. Ample research indicates, however, a somewhat contrary point of view. A lack of attention to broader employee needs has direct negative impacts on organizational effectiveness and the active involvement of individuals and groups in an organization's policy and personnel processes.

Toward Democracy—Administration via Action Research

It appears obvious that other alternative models are needed to avoid those weaknesses noted in the bureaucratic model. We shall provide such a framework by presenting a model of *democracy within administration* as well as of *democracy resulting from administration*.

To do so requires first that we distinguish between two kinds of endeavors: *positivist science* and *action research*. Table 1 provides a useful summary of the major contrasts between positivist science and action research. Much of the previous elaboration on the bureaucratic model clearly may be located on the positivist side of Table 1. Action research, on the other hand, clearly contrasts with the positivist approach since it [28]

> aims to contribute both to the practical concerns of people in an immediate problematic situation and to the goals of social science by joint collaboration within a mutually acceptable ethical framework. Action research is a type of applied social research differing from other varieties in the immediacy of the researcher's involvement in the action process.

The target phenomena and the conditions under which they are studied will determine the analyst's choice of approach. Reliance on positivist science seems contraindicated for designing organizations [29]. Susman and Evered provide more general guidance in this regard by suggesting that [27]

> the researcher ought to be skeptical of positivist science when the unit of analysis is, like the researcher, a self-reflecting subject, when relationships between subjects (actors) are influenced by definitions of the

Table 1 Some Contrasts of Positivist Science and Action Research

Points of comparison	Positivist science	Action research
Value position	Methods are value neutral	Methods develop social systems and release human potential
Time perspective	Observation of the present	Observation of the present plus interpretation of the present from knowledge of the past, conceptualization of more desirable futures
Relationship with units	Detached spectator, client system members are objects to study	Client system members are self-reflective subjects with whom to collaborate
Treatment of units studied	Cases are of interest only as representatives of populations	Cases can be sufficient sources of knowledge
Language for describing units	Denotative, observational	Connotative, metaphorical
Basis for assuming existence of units	Exist independently of human beings	Human artifacts for human purposes
Epistemological aims	Prediction of events from propositions arranged hierarchically	Development of guides for taking actions that produce desired outcomes
Strategy for growth of knowledge	Induction and deduction	Conjecturing, creating settings for learning and modeling of behavior
Criteria for confirmation	Logical consistency, prediction, and control	Evaluating whether actions produce intended consequences
Basis for generalization	Broad, universal, and free of context	Narrow, situational, and bound by context

Source: From Ref. 27.

situation, or when the reason for undertaking the research is to solve a problem which the actors have helped to define.

Basically, as Table 1 suggests, the focus on action research helps reduce the scope of argumentation that historically tended to become polarized into global extremes. Consider the issue of whether or not *principles of administration* exist or can be isolated. The majority of researchers proposed that "universal principles" could be found via a natural science focus if only we had the motivation to proceed with the comprehensive and intense efforts required to isolate them. Critics of this approach had some singular success in creating doubts about the possibilities of identifying or substantiating the existence of administrative principles. Dahl, among others, noted that cultural differences were sufficient to undercut the possibility of any *universal* principles of administration [30].

Such was the momentum of positivist science, however, that although criticism might give pause for reflection, it did not stop the thrust of prevailing opinion. The positions tended to escalate to extremes, avoiding defeat by shifting and enlarging the conceptual battleground but each remaining without victory. At the ideational level contrary results reflected only a truism to true believers, not a rejection: Scientific management could exist nowhere until it existed everywhere.

The notion of action research seeks to borrow from both approaches, in effect, and thereby narrows the character of the debate by focusing on more manageable questions concerning which some tolerable precision is possible. If "universal principles" remain out of reach, for example, is it possible to develop approaches and technologies for dealing effectively with limited but still common problem situations? Illustratively, given that some naturally occurring social systems tend to generate some quite specific and more desirable consequences at work than others, it is possible to use such knowledge to help induce the planned development of specific norms and behaviors at some site that would increase the proportion of desired outcomes *there?* In this basic sense, action research is value loaded from the outset, in sharp contrast to positivist science.

Put briefly, action research does not fixate on universal principles. Rather, it focuses on what may be called *contingent regularities*, with the preferences of immediate actors and their ownership of action plans being among the major contingencies. Note, however, that action research implies a profundity that can become a snare and a delusion if pushed too far. Action research seeks to emphasize the role of what might be called *structures of consciousness* through the direct involvement of the *subjects of study*, including the researcher. This is also in sharp contrast with positivist science, which calls for sharp distinctions between *objective* and *subjective* reality and the arms-length treatment of the objects of study. As Brown notes [31]:

> Organization realities are not external to human consciousness, out there waiting to be recorded. Instead, the world as humans know it is constituted intersubjectively. The faces (facta) of this world are things made. They are neither subjective nor objective in the usual sense. Instead, they are construed through a process of symbolic interaction. A revision of our symbolic structures, of our shared forms of perception and expression, is thus a revisioning of the world.

The view that social life can be in critical respects a conscious process of world creation implies both great leverage over and awesome responsibility for our human condition. Action research often deals with *social reality*, the ways and shapes in which experience acquires significance. As Brown concludes [31], it

> provides a bridge between theoretical and organizational praxis, as well as between what experts do and what workers do in their workday lives. We all create worlds. The more we are able to create worlds that are morally cogent and politically viable, the more we are able, as workers and as citizens, to manage or resist.

Perspectives on OD as a Value-Loaded Approach

The focus on OD as value loaded is not lightly chosen. The inadequacies of the democracy-versus-administration model stem to a substantial degree from its neglect of values as well as from the casual assumption that managerial techniques could be somehow freed from underlying values or cultures. OD reflects an almost totally reversed set of underlying premises.

OD is value loaded in broad concept. It was initially seen as a philosophy-cum-learning design for moving toward the creation of appropriate societies and cultures at the worksite (see Ref. 4, Part 1, pp. 1–190). OD more specifically provides shape and form for social and cultural reconstruction by prescribing such values as [32]:

Full and free communication,
Greater reliance on open confrontation in managing conflict, where participants psychologically own at least the causes of the conflict and its consequences as well as (hopefully) agree on approaches to managing the conflict,
Influence based on competence rather than on personal whim or formal power,

Expression of emotional as well as task-oriented behavior.
Acceptance of conflict between the individual and the organization to be
coped with willingly, openly, and rationally.

These few prescriptions are clearly analogous to democratic ideals and
suggest that OD implies a far different social and cultural context for work
than do bureaucratic principles.

OD is also value loaded in its constituent designs. OD designs are often
described in technical or helping terms, but they are nonetheless rooted in
distinct values that typically have power and political implications sharply distinguished from the values associated with the bureaucratic model. A
central feature of OD designs, for example, involves the sharing of valid
and reliable information as compared to the centralizing tendencies of the
bureaucracy. Smith, with good reason, emphasizes the political character
and consequences of the apparently simple and generally appealing prescription for "open" interaction in organizations [33].

In addition, the value-loaded and political features of broader OD interventions loom even larger. Consider the use of empirical research in
organization change. Empirical research may tell us which structural arrangements are more likely to be associated with high productivity and
worker satisfaction. However, even if a comprehensive organizational
theory were available, the choice of a structural alternative and its implementation require a choice between values and the activation of processes that may broadly be called "political" [34] and whose thrust is clearly more democratic than the principles.

OD Designs for Moving toward Democracy within and through Administration

How, then, should one move toward democracy in administration
through the use of OD? Reason encourages caution, expects incremental
advances as our knowledge and experience increase, and prescribes focusing on selected activities in those organizations that are experiencing sufficient trauma to help motivate change and to heighten the probablity of
successful implementation. The action research orientation of OD implies
major constraints on its being seen as just another utopian ideology.

Some OD interventions require *limited purpose contracts*—e.g., flexible work hours and third-party consultation often seem to do quite nicely
with little prework for the development of appropriate attitudes, skills,
and cultures [35]. Other OD interventions may require substantial prework. For example, career planning requires not only a supportive socio-

emotional culture but also appropriate management practices and policies such as those related to the possibility that an individual might modify unsatisfying conditions related to a job, including the restructuring of work and its supervision. A useful design feature of a career planning package involves an analysis of the positive and negative aspects of a person's job. As one of the final tasks, individuals are instructed to choose as a change target some undesirable aspects of their job, within general policy guidelines and with the help of peers and often a consultant. The individual chooses an aspect of work, plans to ameliorate it, seeks to implement that plan, and reports back to a group of cocareer planners. In addition to the benefits which come from careful prework efforts, the process signals commitment to the proposition that, in the long run, a high and growing congruence between individual needs and organization requirements is a major goal (see Ref. 4, Part 1, pp. 203–225).

Beyond such introductory notions about moving toward democracy *within* and *through* administration, two basic approaches come to mind. Ways and means have to be developed to directly energize multiple forms or levels of democracy within organizations. In addition, complementary efforts must be made toward the development of what might be called *useful supports* for nonauthoritarian behavior in organizations. The basic challenge can be presented in the following manner:

$$\text{Energize multiple levels} \atop \text{of democracy} \leftrightarrow \text{Provide attitudinal and behavioral} \atop \text{supports}$$

Energize Multiple Levels of Democracy. The first aspect of the challenge of moving toward Administration III involves energizing the several levels of democracy within the organizational setting. Numerous available OD designs variously relate to these levels. To illustrate, we use Dahl's four forms of democracy [3] and add an individual level:

Individual values and democratic forms	Applicable OD designs
Enhanced individual freedom and responsibility	Flexible work hours Career planning
Committee democracy, in which all members have a more or less equal say while in face-to-face contact	Team building Sensitivity training with intact work teams

Referendum democracy, in which all views are represented, although individuals do not necessarily speak out themselves	Interview/feedback Survey/feedback Group confrontations
Representative democracy, in which some smaller selected group speaks out for a larger collectivity	Group decision making Joint labor/management committee for quality of working life efforts Large agenda- and norm-setting meetings with diverse participants from various levels of one or more organizations
Polyarchical democracy, which includes the forms above and also provides roles for diverse interest groups and for complex delegations of authority	Collective bargaining and other labor/management interaction that focus on QWL as well as pay and fringes [36]

Three significant points may be made as to how OD designs can energize the several forms or levels of democracy. First, and most evident, much available OD practice can be catalogued in terms of the forms of democracy.

Second, OD designs tend to cluster in the "more democratic" forms; that is, experience basically relates to the general enhancement of individual freedom and responsibility as well as to organizational analogs of what Dahl referred to as committee and referendum democracy. Team building in small work units [37], for example, can be extended to large numbers of individuals in the same organization by arranging for numerous iterations of a similar design in many work teams at various levels as well as by holding various interface or integrative meetings to test and reinforce learning. Hundreds of individuals (or even more) in work teams can be exposed—in series, as it were—to team building designs to help induce appropriate norms, behaviors, and attitudes [38]. Typically, the focus is on improving the quality of the communication processes—as by increasing trust, reducing risk, and increasing openness and owning—which in turn may later lead to technical and substantive improvements in work team performance. The learned behavior in small groups may then be tested in interface experiences as teams confront a common superior after having spent considerable time in developing appropriate attitudes or skills [39] or as culturally prepared teams seek to develop or enhance relations with other teams in a flow-of-work design (see Ref. 4, Part 2, pp. 138–152).

Opinion polling methods may also be coupled with OD designs using face-to-face interaction. Whereas team building percolates up, these survey/feedback designs also variously trickle down. Even when large populations are involved, it is possible to disaggregate data for use at numerous organizational levels for in-depth analysis [40]. Survey/feedback may, in a sense, be thought of as a complex combination of referendum democracy followed by committee democracy. By employing statistical techniques that isolate comparative trends in various smaller subgroups, survey/feedback designs also seek to improve socioemotional and task aspects of work. The survey captures the moods and attitudes of organization members about various aspects of the work site. Hopefully, the revealed data will activate energies in the subgroups to begin doing something specific about those moods and attitudes through action planning meetings [41]. Finally, since sampling methods can make periodic polling quite painless, large systems can, in effect, maintain real-time programs of pulse taking, which, in turn, could trigger action planning.

At the representative democracy level, OD experience and theory are thinner. Coch and French's classic experiment with alternate forms of decision making implies the virtues of direct representation of employees in work-site decisions [42]. More recently, joint labor/management committees at the plant level have been used to help improve the quality of work life. And some experience with large agenda- and norm-setting meetings indicates that individual OD designs can impact on large numbers of individuals in short time frames (see Ref. 4, Part 2, pp. 134–136).

Third, at the polyarchical democracy level, it is perhaps best to say that the form and character of OD efforts are yet to be determined. In many European countries, code termination by labor and management at macro levels constitutes perhaps the most ambitious expression of interest. Little American interest has been expressed in such macro arrangements until recently. American unions have traditionally focused on wages and fringes and, with few exceptions, have shown only episodic interest in working conditions and far less in the comanagement or codirection of work. In smaller systems, to be sure, experience with polyarchical approaches is growing, with schools providing perhaps the most fertile field [43] for experimentation. Other efforts include the various approaches to involving the "underrepresenteds"—as via an ombudsman for consumers or clients of governmental services or various public affairs departments inside business corporations who serve as devil's advocates for consumer viewpoints that might otherwise not be given effective or regular voice.

Provide Useful Attitudinal and Behavioral Supports. Energizing the several levels of democracy implies successful efforts to build appropriate attitudinal and behavioral supports. Often this process will take place in OD designs such as those involving team building, survey/feedback, etc. In other instances, such supports will derive from a variety of more focused learning designs as well as from specific institutional and structural arrangements.

Figure 3 shows four classes of such supports along with a sampling of relevant OD designs. Not all of these designs will necessarily be relevant in a specific organization at a particular time, and, of course, some organizations might do well enough without any of them. In short, accurate diagnosis is of critical importance in determining the applicability of any design. Generally, however, such designs seem to have special attractions in certain kinds of organizations. Included in such a list would be those with multiple product lines or programs, with a major technological component, under conditions of high turbulence and change, and/or with a skilled and professionalized work force. It should be noted, however, that many designs have proven generally useful in a wide range of organizations under diverse conditions (see Ref. 4, Parts 1 and 2).

When discussing *organizational opportunities for individual choice*, appropriate designs can cover a broad range. Some are conceptually simple and can be implemented with modest skill and sparse commitment of resources under broad ranges of organizational conditions. Programs of flexible work hours illustrate this class of designs, and their useful effects get massive support from both the private and public sectors [44]. Other designs anchor the opposite end of a scale of resources/skills/commitments. Career planning typifies OD designs of the latter type and postulates that, in the long run, neither the individual nor the organization will profit from individuals being in roles whose demands substantially exceed an individual's skills or expectations. Working through such subtle balancing requires substantial commitments from individuals and their organizations. One of the most significant facets of career planning involves a recognition of stages of both individual and organizational development as well as responses to them [45].

As for the common need to develop *necessary attitudes and behavioral skills*, it is obvious that opportunities for individual choice will not necessarily be taken advantage of. Increasing the probability of such outcomes will depend substantially on the availability of appropriate skills and attitudes which support increased individual choice making.

Appropriate designs here also cover a wide range. Some attitudes and

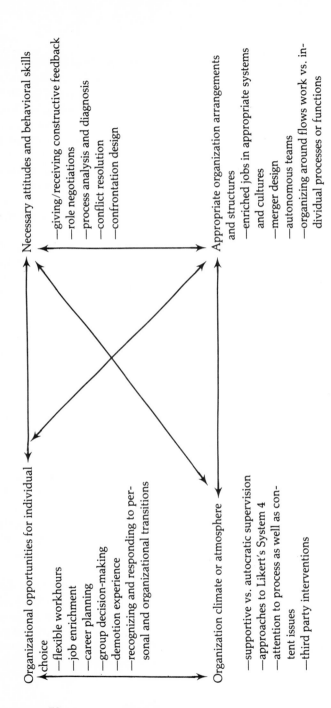

Organizational opportunities for individual choice

—flexible workhours
—job enrichment
—career planning
—group decision-making
—demotion experience
—recognizing and responding to personal and organizational transitions

Necessary attitudes and behavioral skills

—giving/receiving constructive feedback
—role negotiations
—process analysis and diagnosis
—conflict resolution
—confrontation design

Organization climate or atmosphere

—supportive vs. autocratic supervision
—approaches to Likert's System 4
—attention to process as well as content issues
—third party interventions

Appropriate organization arrangements and structures

—enriched jobs in appropriate systems and cultures
—merger design
—autonomous teams
—organizing around flows work vs. individual processes or functions

Figure 3 Arraying OD designs by four major classes of attitudinal and behavioral supports

behavioral skills are quite generic—such as those associated with giving and receiving constructive feedback or with active listening—and will be more or less relevant at all stages of individual and organizational development. Other designs will be of more limited usefulness, e.g., role negotiation [46].

Opportunities plus appropriate attitudes and behavioral skills constitute powerful motivation to make choices and to accept the consequences. But experience indicates that *organization climate or atmosphere* will play a dominant role in influencing whether even individuals with appropriate attitudes and skills will take advantage of available opportunities. Even strong preferences and major opportunities may be thwarted by the admonition "That just isn't done around here."

OD experience provides substantial support regarding the significance of organization climate or atmosphere, especially in regard to pitfalls which should be avoided [47]. Available designs include discrete efforts to modify supervisory styles [48] as well as to influence broad patterns of interpersonal and group relationships [39]. In general, experience implies that simultaneous attacks from both directions work best. Indeed, attempts to modify supervisory styles without inducing an appropriate social or cultural context may not only fail but may prove seriously counterproductive. At the same time, creating broad social expectations for individuals who lack appropriate behavioral skills may also be ill-advised.

The final class of multiple reinforcers in this analysis—often the most important in practice—includes various *organizational arrangements and structures* for work, following Model II [49]. This approach is often overlooked in OD. Indeed, by far, the dominant interventions involve interaction-centered designs—those related to attitudes and behavioral skills as well as to climates and atmospheres. Such interventions can initially seem to succeed and then suddenly "fade out" in the absence of appropriate changes in the manner in which work is structured. For example, organizations departmentalized by functions will tend to encourage an authoritarian style of supervision. A careless superimposition of OD designs supporting nonauthoritarian attitudes and behaviors on such an organization can be seriously traumatic, especially when the move is attempted in one big jump by means of interaction-centered designs without corresponding changes in the organization of work or in its supporting culture [47].

Some research exists in appropriate structural form, with job enrichment having received the most attention. Care should be exercised, however, especially because a Band-Aid type of approach tends to dominate current practice, whereas a more systemic view should prevail. More

specifically, job enrichment programs ill-suit organizations with a bureaucratic structure. Numerous failures of job enrichment qua technique have
been reported [50], and many of these failures may be attributed to an in-
appropriate systemic culture and structure for enlarged jobs. The following contrast illustrates the point:

Bureaucratic structures imply	Job enrichment implies
Authoritarian supervision	Supportive supervision
Monitoring details of performance	Monitoring overall performance
Limiting employees to a single opera-tion or few operations in a total se-quence	Control by employees of a total se-quence of operations
Separating a worker from control of work	Integrating a worker and control of work
Centralizing decision making re. op-erations	Decentralizing decision making re. operations

Conclusion

This movement toward democracy *within* and *through* administration
represents a search for a useful middle ground. The poles of argument
seem clear enough. Thus Mosher cautions that " . . . democracy within administration, *if carried to the full,* raises a logical dilemma in its relation to
political democracy" [51]. In this chapter we have suggested that bureaucracy within administration also raises logical and practical dilemmas in
relation to political democracy as well as efficient and effective administration. We have proposed that the influences of bureaucratic life within
the organization go far beyond the organization to condition the individual's role in the broader political culture. In the present view, OD is seen as
permitting the exploration of a needed middle ground which offers a greater likelihood of meeting individual needs and organizational demands and
supporting democratic values in the political culture.

References

1. Robert T. Golembiewski, "The Ideational Poverty of Two Modes of
   Coupling Democracy and Administration," *International Journal of
   Public Administration,* 38 (January 1981):1–65.

2. Emmette S. Redford, *Democracy in the Administrative State*, Oxford University Press, New York, 1969, pp. 70–71.
3. Robert A. Dahl, *After the Revolution?*, Yale University Press, New Haven, 1975, p. 94.
4. Robert T. Golembiewski (ed.), *Approaches to Planned Change*, Parts 1 and 2, Dekker, New York, 1979.
5. *Work in America*, M.I.T. Press, Cambridge, Mass., 1973.
6. Leonard R. Sayles and Margaret Chandler, *Managing Large Systems*, Harper & Row, New York, 1971.
7. Herbert C. Kelman, "Processes of Opinion Change," *Public Opinion Quarterly*, 25 (Spring 1961):57–78.
8. Warren G. Bennis, "Organizations of the Future," *Personnel Administration*, 30 (September 1967):6–19.
9. Robert T. Golembiewski, "Civil Service and Managing Work," *American Political Science Review*, 56 (December 1962):961–973.
10. Robert L. Peabody and Francis Rourke, "Public Bureaucracies," in James G. March (ed.), *Handbook of Organizations*, Rand McNally, Skokie, Ill., 1965, pp. 807, 810, 813, 816.
11. Bruce Buchanan, "Government Managers, Business Executives, and Organizational Commitment," *Public Administration Review*, 34 (July 1979):339–347.
12. Hal G. Rainey, "Perceptions of Incentives in Business and Government: Implications for Civil Service Reform," *Public Administration Review*, 39 (September 1979):440–447.
13. Frank T. Paine, Stephen J. Carroll, Jr., and Burt A. Leete, "Need Satisfactions of Managerial Level Personnel in a Government Agency," *Journal of Applied Psychology*, 50 (June 1966):247–249.
14. Jesse B. Rhinehart, R. P. Barrell, A. S. De Wolfe, J. E. Griffin, and F. E. Spaner, "Comparative Study of Need Satisfactions in Governmental and Business Hierarchies," *Journal of Applied Psychology*, 53 (June 1969):230–235.
15. Frederick Thayer, "The President's Management 'Reforms,' " *Public Administration Review*, 38 (July 1978):309–314.
16. Lisl Klein, *New Forms of Work Organization*, Cambridge University Press, Cambridge, 1976, p. 30.
17. Sidney Verba, *Small Groups and Political Behavior*, Princeton University Press, Princeton, N.J., 1961, pp. 30–60.
18. Michael Maccoby, "Changing Work," *Working Papers*, 2 (1975).
19. Max Elden, "Political Efficacy at Work," paper presented for the Seminar on Social Change and Organization Development, Inter-University Center for Graduate Studies, Dubrovnik, Yugoslavia, 1977.

82   *Golembiewski*

20. Robert Ford, *Motivation in the Work Itself*, American Management Association, New York, 1969.
21. Richard Walton, "Work Innovations at Topeka," *Journal of Applied Behavioral Science*, 13 (July 1977):422–433.
22. Einar Thorsrud, *Model for Socio-Technical Systems*, Work Research Institutes, Oslo, 1976.
23. Robert T. Golembiewski, *Men, Management, and Morality*, McGraw-Hill, New York, 1965.
24. W. McWhinney, "Open Systems—Traditional Hierarchies," paper presented at Quality of Working Life Conference, Arden House, New York, 1972.
25. Max Elden, "Democracy at Work for More Participatory Politics," unpublished doctoral dissertation, University of California at Los Angeles, 1976.
26. Paul H. Appleby, *Morality and Administration In Democratic Government*, Lousiana State University Press, Baton Rouge, 1952.
27. Gerald I. Susman and Roger D. Evered, "An Assessment of the Scientific Merits of Action Research," *Administrative Science Quarterly*, 23 (December 1978):582–603.
28. Comprehensively, see Newton Margulies and Anthony P. Raia, *Conceptual Foundations of Organizational Development*, McGraw-Hill, New York, 1978, p. 63.
29. Peter B. Vaill, "The Expository Model of Science in Organization Design," in Ralph H. Kilmann, Louis R. Pondy, and Dennis P. Slevin (eds.), *The Management of Organization Design*, Elsevier North-Holland, New York, 1976.
30. Robert A. Dahl, "The Science of Public Administration," *Public Administration Review*, 7 (Winter 1947):1–11.
31. Richard Harvey Brown, "Bureaucracy as Praxis: Toward a Political Phenomenology of Formal Organizations," *Administrative Science Quarterly*, 23 (September 1978):365–382.
32. Philip A. Slater and Warren G. Bennis, "Democracy Is Inevitable," *Harvard Business Review*, 42 (March 1964):51–59.
33. Ken K. Smith, "A Political Perspective on Openness"; See Ref. 4.
34. Virginia E. Schein, "Political Strategies for Implementing Organizational Change," *Group and Organization Studies*, 2 (March 1977): 42–48.
35. Robert T. Golembiewski and Carl W. Proehl, Jr., "Public Sector Applications of Flexible Workhours," *Public Administration Review*, 40 (January 1980):72–85.
36. Paul G. Goodman, *Assessing Organizational Change*, Wiley-Inter-

science, New York, 1979.

37. William G. Dyer, *Team-Building,* Addison-Wesley, Reading, Mass., 1977.
38. Reuben T. Harris and Jerry L. Porras, "The Consequences of Large System Change in Practice," in Jeffrey C. Susbauer (ed.), *Proceedings,* 1978 Annual Meeting, San Francisco, August 1978, Academy of Management, pp. 298–302.
39. Robert T. Golembiewski and Stokes B. Carrigan, "Planned Change in Organization Style Based on Laboratory Approach," *Administrative Science Quarterly,* 15 (September 1970):330–340.
40. Robert T. Golembiewski and Richard Hilles, *Toward the Responsive Organization,* Brighton, Salt Lake City, 1979.
41. David A. Nadler, *Feedback and Organization Development,* Addison-Wesley, Reading, Mass., 1977.
42. Lester Coch and John R. P. French, Jr., "Overcoming Resistance to Change," *Human Relations,* 1 (1948):512–532.
43. Richard A. Schmuck, et al., *Consultation for Innovative Schools,* Center for Educational Policy and Management, Eugene, Ore., 1975.
44. Robert T. Golembiewski, Ronald Fox, and Carl W. Proehl, Jr., "Is Flexi-Time 'Hard Time' for Supervisors?: Two Sources of Data Rejecting the Proposition," *Journal of Management,* 5 (Fall 1979):241–259.
45. Robert T. Golembiewski, "Mid-life Transition and Mid-career Crisis," *Public Administration Review,* 38 (May 1978):215–222.
46. Roger Harrison, "Role Negotiation," in Robert T. Golembiewski and William Eddy (eds.), *Organization Development in Public Administration,* Dekker, New York, 1978, pp. 178–190.
47. Per-Olof Berg, *Emotional Structures in Organizations,* Student-literatur, Lund, 1979.
48. Edward Fleishman, "Leadership Climate, Human Relations Training and Supervisory Behavior," *Personnel Psychology,* 6 (Summer 1953): 205–222.
49. Robert T. Golembiewski, "Infusing Organizations with OD Values: Public-Sector Approaches to Structural Change," *Southern Review of Public Administration,* 4 (December 1980):269–302.
50. Linda L. Frank and J. Richard Hackman, "A Failure of Job Enrichment," *Journal of Applied Behavioral Science,* 11 (October 1976): 413–436.
51. Frederick Mosher, *Democracy and Public Service,* Oxford University Press, New York, 1968, p. 374.

4

The Impact of NASPAA's Standards on Defining the Field of Public Administration

Daniel M. Poore *
The Pennsylvania State University, Capitol Campus,
Middletown, Pennsylvania

Education for public administration has lacked a common professional focus since its origins in the early 1900s. In recent years the field has been experiencing a crisis of identity of both an intellectual and curricular nature. Students and employers have been bewildered by the extreme diversity in educational philosophy and curricular content of programs calling themselves public administration. During the 1970s, the National Association of Schools of Public Affairs and Administration (NASPAA) took a number of actions aimed at improving education for public administration. In 1974, guidelines and standards for master's programs were approved, and in 1977, standards and a national peer review process for master's programs were approved.

A basic purpose of NASPAA's efforts in developing standards is to create a more coherent identity for the field by seeking a consensus on its nature, breadth, and common base of knowledge and skills. If NASPAA's efforts are successful, the standards should have the following impacts on defining the field of public administration: (1) broad acceptance of public administration as a field of multidisciplinary professional education; (2) recognition that with good program design a very broad array of public functions or specialties under the public administration umbrella can be a strength; (3) eventual acceptance of a set of general knowledge, abilities, and skills as a common base for all programs; and (4) program designs

---

*The author is currently affiliated with Coastal Carolina College, University of South Carolina, Conway, South Carolina.

providing strong means–ends linkages between common core components and advanced work.

Introduction

The National Association of Schools of Public Affairs and Administration (NASPAA) is a professional education association whose primary purpose is to promote high standards of performance in education for public administration [1]. My intent in this chapter is to discuss the recent and continuing efforts by NASPAA to develop program standards and attempt to explain the impact that these standards are intended to have on defining the academic field of public administration.

Public administration programs have been characterized more by their extreme diversity in educational philosophy and curricula than by a common professional focus. As noted by Dwight Waldo [2]:

Far from representing a coherent and well-agreed upon educational philosophy and program, it [NASPAA] represents a wide variety of philosophies and contains programs with a wide variety of titles, contents, and objectives.

This lack of a common professional focus reflects the changing perceptions of and the conflicting opinions about the nature and substance of public administration that have persisted since its origins in the early 1900s. The literature contains many articles and essays dealing with the "identity crisis" and the "intellectual crisis" of public administration [3]. Neither a generally accepted theoretic base nor firm boundaries for the field have ever existed.

The 1974 NASPAA Guidelines and Standards

In 1974, only 4 years after its creation, NASPAA's membership took the first step toward providing a better definition of the field of public administration by adopting a set of guidelines and standards at the annual meeting in Syracuse [4]. These guidelines were designed to encourage master's degree programs to develop a professional focus in contrast to a liberal arts focus, to include a matrix of professional competencies in their curricula, and to feature the attributes of public service management as distinguished from private business management. This decision by NASPAA's member programs placed the association in a leadership role for developing and improving education for public management. A strong factor prompting this action was a 1973 report by Chapman and Cleaveland, which concluded that "current programs of education for public administration are not meeting present professional needs and, without considerable rejuvenation, most certainly will fail to meet the needs of tomorrow's public service" [5].

Of particular concern to NASPAA's membership was the bewilderment expressed by potential students and employers over the wide variation in curricular content of master's degree programs using the title *public administration*. The problems and concerns are summarized in Appendix A of NASPAA's guidelines and standards. They include the profuse variation previously mentioned, the threat of a "cheap" professional degree in public administration, the lack of professional focus, the proliferation of courses and program specializations, the increasing dissatisfaction of employing agencies, and the lack of status as a professional field vis-à-vis other professions in the public service [6].

The guidelines and standards approved in 1974 were prescriptive only to the extent that they provided goals for the improvement of programs. Particular emphasis was placed on fostering a professional focus for master's programs and providing graduates with specific competencies for management in the public sector. Programs were encouraged to remodel their curricula around a "matrix of professional competencies" [7], which consists of knowledge, skills, public interest values, and behavior in five major subject matter areas: (1) political, social, and economic context; (2) analytical tools, both quantitative and nonquantitative; (3) individual, groups, and organizational dynamics; (4) policy analysis; and (5) administrative/management processes.

In addition, guidelines were provided for length of program, composition and qualifications of faculty, student admission policies, program organization and jurisdiction, and facilities. In this chapter I am concerned only with those matters that are expected to have an impact on how the academic field of public administration will be defined in the future.

During 1975, 39 NASPAA member schools prepared and submitted self-study reports to NASPAA comparing the various aspects of their master's programs with the guidelines and standards for master's degrees. In 1976, the NASPAA Standards Committee initiated a review process for these self-study reports [8]. Twenty-nine faculty members from a wide cross section of NASPAA schools reviewed 15 of the reports and provided their comments to the standards committee. All 39 of the reports were read by at least two members of the committee. The results of this review process served to clarify and reemphasize the problems and concerns confronting education for public administration. They can be summarized in two key issues: (1) the need for a strong professional focus and (2) the need for general agreement on a set of common knowledge and skills. These issues are vital to defining the field of public administration.

Need for Professional Focus in Public Administration

The master's program in public administration has long been considered to be a professional-type degree. As defined by Alice and Donald Stone [9]:

> Professional education in public administration is concerned with application, operations, and performance, not primarily with theory, abstractions, and research methodology. It draws on all relevant disciplines and professions in developing the insights and the skills needed to plan, determine policy, organize, manage, and implement programs and operations.

But there is disagreement over whether public administration is a discipline, a field, or a profession. Part of the argument seems to revolve around the nature of the actual practice of public administration in government. While endorsing the need for a strong professional focus in graduate education for public administration, I do not intend to imply that the practice of public administration is now or is ever likely to become a true profession. Indeed, I agree with Don K. Price, who contends that a hard distinction will continue to exist between the true professional and the administrator [10]. However, I do not share Richard L. Schott's concern over NASPAA's use of the term *professional* in attempting to improve education for public administration [11]. It behooves public administration to take on certain characteristics of a profession, even though it is not likely ever to become one.

Both Waldo and Frederickson agree that public administration is certainly not an academic discipline [12]. Waldo proposed that [13]:

> we try to act as a profession without actually being one, and perhaps even w⁊ .hout the hope or intention of becoming one in any strict sense. . . . The professional perspective or stance is the only one broad and flexible enough to enable us to contain our diverse interests and objectives, yet firm and understanding enough to provide some unity and sense of direction and purpose.

Most certainly public administration may best be characterized as a multidisciplinary field, which attempts to integrate and apply theory from vari-

ous disciplines to the problems of making and implementing public policy.
I do not agree with Schick's view that "the seeking after professional
recognition is an effort to establish an identify apart from political science
rather than a means of accommodating to the diversities within the field"
[14]. The study of political processes obviously has a major role in public
policy analysis, but so should economics, psychology, sociology, and
some of the hard sciences. But with regard to its contribution to effective
administration, the role of political science theory has not been particularly strong. In my view, the integration and application of a variety of disciplines to a particular line of endeavor has a legitimate role in its own right,
which is more nearly like that of a profession than like any traditional
academic discipline.

Schott has observed that professionalism arises basically from a specialized technique acquired by extended training [15]. This implies that for
public administration education to become more professional in nature, it
must embody a set of common knowledge and skills which are basic ingredients for the effective analysis and implementation of public policy. This
is one of the primary purposes of the NASPAA standards.

The review of the 1975 self-study reports brought forth such a diversity
of program missions, degree requirements, and curricular content that it
would be farfetched to classify education for public administration
generally as a professional field. A few programs have had a strong professional focus for many years, and others have undoubtedly progressed in
that direction since 1975, but a long and possibly rocky road still lies ahead
in professionalizing graduate education for public administration.

The development of a strong professional focus appears to be directly
related to who exercises jurisdictional control over the program goals, the
selection of the faculty, and the design of the curriculum. If the traditional
liberal arts viewpoint is dominant among those in control, then the development of a strong professional focus is quite doubtful. At many institutions the question of jurisdictional control over the public administration
program is quite sensitive and not easy to change. This is particularly true
in those situations where a public administration program is subordinate
to a political science faculty. The review of the self-study reports indicates
that a strong relationship exists between the organizational autonomy of a
program within its institution and the strength of its professional focus. In
other words, when master's programs have strong organizational identity
and considerable jurisdictional control over their faculty, curriculum, and
budget, they appear to have a more professional and public-service-ori-
ented character.

Need for a Set of Common Knowledge and Skills

An extremely broad range of subject matter content and degree requirements existed among the 39 programs studied in 1976. The minimum degree requirements varied from 30 semester credits with no undergraduate prerequisites specified to 60 semester credits spread over 2 years. There were very few recognizable common core subjects among all programs. While there may be strength in some diversity, such extreme diversity cannot lead to the recognition of public administration as a strong professional field.

It appeared that only a few programs had made any serious attempts to compare their curricula with NASPAA's matrix of professional competencies. Those who did try employed widely varying interpretations of the meaning of the matrix. This was not really surprising, though, because the matrix covers such a broad array of knowledge, skills, values, and behavior that it would not be realistic to include it all in any depth in a single master's program. The matrix is really a guide to the continuing education of public managers, rather than the basis for a common body of knowledge and skills for master's degree programs. Accordingly, faculties found it difficult to compare program curricula with the maxtrix. This led to a tendency for faculties to pick and choose subjects from the matrix based on their interests and preferences, rather than to regard the matrix as a common base for curriculum development.

It was apparent that most programs were weak in at least one area of the matrix. Policy-oriented programs tended to be weak in organizational dynamics and administration/management processes, whereas management-oriented programs appeared to be weak in political processes and basic policy analysis. A general weakness appeared to exist in economics and quantitative tools. The need for agreement on a set of common curriculum components and minimum degree requirements become very apparent if the goal of professional education is ever to be achieved.

Development of Standards and a Peer Review Process

As a result of reviewing the 39 self-study reports, the NASPAA Standards Committee concluded that a more direct and concise statement of standards for master's programs would be necessary for achieving the purpose of significantly improving the quality and professional focus of public affairs/public administration programs. The committee proceeded to develop a set of standards using the 1974 guidelines and standards as a foundation [16]. The proposed standards were thoroughly discussed and revised in several open sessions at NASPAA's 1977 annual conference in Colorado Springs, before being approved by the membership at the business meeting on the final day of the conference.

Concurrent with the effort to develop standards, NASPAA's long-range-goals task force was investigating the desirability of providing some means for evaluating the quality of master's degrees offered by member institutions. The options ranged from peer review comment on written self-study reports to a full accreditation process. As a result of hearings held in various parts of the country during 1976–1977, the task force decided to recommend a voluntary process involving self-study reports, site visits, a determination as to whether or not programs are in substantial conformance with NASPAA standards, and the publication of the names of the approved programs. This voluntary peer review process, which is not formal accreditation but very similar to it, was adopted by the NASPAA membership along with the standards at the 1977 annual meeting. Such a process is essential if the standards are to have any substantial impact on defining the field of public administration.

The debate at Colorado Springs and at the prior hearings of the long-range-goals task force was intense and often heated. The focus of the debate was not directed primarily at the content of the standards themselves but rather at the peer review process, which strongly resembles accreditations in other professional fields. The major argument against moving toward a system of informal accreditation involved the fear that such action would give NASPAA sufficient power to bring programs into line with the standards, with the result being the stifling of creativity and diversity in program curricula and delivery. As Birkhead has observed, "This is the vision of the dead hand of uniformity that critics of the accreditation process and some critics of standards fear" [17].

The uniformity argument had been recognized as a legitimate concern by the standards committee during the development of the standards. The need to build flexibility into the standards became the guiding force behind the development of the two-tier concept for the curriculum aspects of the standards. The first tier requires a common body of basic knowledge and skills, while the second tier allows wide latitude in designing advanced curriculum areas. It seems very unlikely to me that NASPAA's efforts to agree on a common body of basic knowledge and skills as the basis for professional education in public administration will result in undesirable program uniformity. It is more likely to produce the hoped for result of improving the capability of master's program graduates to engage in intelligent analysis and implementation of public sector programs. The process of peer review and perhaps eventual accreditation might conceivably inhibit program faculties from experimenting with new curricular and teaching ideas. It behooves the membership of NASPAA to zealously guard against any perceived trends toward the development of too much program uniformity and the stifling of new ideas and approaches while at the same time strengthening education for public administration.

Letters of intent to participate in the first cycle of peer review were submitted by 85 NASPAA programs. By the July 1979 deadline, 67 master's programs had submitted their self-study reports to the NASPAA Peer Review Committee for participation in the first cycle of peer review.

The first roster of 45 approved programs was released by NASPAA during the summer of 1980. The peer review committee had judged these 45 master's programs to be in substantial conformity with NASPAA's standards. There are undoubtedly other programs which satisfy the standards but which chose not to enter the first cycle of peer review.

The second cycle of peer review began in September 1980. NASPAA's plans call for repeating the process and updating the roster of approved programs on an annual basis for the foreseeable future. It will take several years before the real impact of NASPAA's standards on education for public administration can be determined. However, the first cycle of peer review in 1979–1980 revealed that many progams have undertaken considerable curriculum redesign based on the standards since the approval of the standards in 1977. If the peer review process is maintained diligently by NASPAA over a period of years, then the standards should make a significant impact on the definition of public administration as a field of professional education.

The Intended Impact of NASPAA'S Standards

NASPAA's efforts in developing program standards and a peer review process are intended to establish a clearer definition of the field. In this attempt, considerable care has been taken to encourage flexibility and innovation in curriculum design and program implementation. While seeking a common focus, the standards are not intended to put the field into a straitjacket, as some critics have implied. Rather, their purpose is to foster greatly needed improvements in education for public administration. In this regard, NASPAA's standards for master's programs were designed to provide program direction in the following areas: (1) multidisciplinary professional education, (2) breadth of the field, (3) a set of common curriculum components, and (4) advanced work or specialty areas.

Multidisciplinary Professional Education

In adopting the standards, NASPAA's member programs have agreed to vigorously pursue the goal of bringing a strong professional focus to the field of public administration. The goal of professional education is woven into the fabric of the standards in many places. Standard 1.2 emphasizes that the standards apply only to programs whose purpose is to provide professional education. Standard 2.2 strengthens this point by limiting eligibility for the peer review to programs which are committed to professional education in public policy and administration as their primary objective. Programs having a traditional liberal arts orientation, with a strong single discipline focus, are discouraged from entering the peer review process.

Standard 3.0 is aimed at encouraging sufficient organizational jurisdiction or autonomy for public administration faculties so that they may effectively plan and implement a professional program. No specific form of organization is required by this standard, but the public administration unit is expected to have effective jurisdiction over curriculum requirements, course scheduling, admission of students, certification of degree candidates, and a program budget, along with participation in the appointment and promotion of the unit's faculty. The test of whether the public administration unit has effective jurisdiction is best seen in the nature of the curriculum offerings and the professional orientation of the faculty.

Standard 3.0, program jurisdiction, generated considerable debate at Colorado Springs because it hits at the heart of the issue of developing a multidiscipline professional approach for public administration versus a single-discipline liberal arts orientation. This has been a particularly vexing issue because at least 50 percent of the MPA programs in existence have had their origins in a department of political science. The motivation for the development of many of these programs sprang more from declining enrollments in political science than from a strong desire to offer a professional program. As a result, many programs were professional in name only, with their substance and flavor coming primarily from political science. As long as the effective control of these programs remained in the hands of political science faculty, it was not likely that a truly professional focus would evolve. During the debate, Standard 3.0 was modified to the effect that no particular form of program organization is required. However, the intent remains that the professional MPA faculty should have jurisdiction over the program.

Standard 4.0 requires that the curriculum be designed to prepare professionals who are oriented toward effective action in the public sector, rather than toward research and teaching. As a necessary complement to this, Standard 5.0 stipulates that the qualitative adequacy of the faculty shall include professional experience and public service as well as the traditionally expected earned doctorate and research and publication. In addition, it encourages the use of well-qualified practicing professionals for teaching in their areas of special expertise.

The trend toward professionalism in public administration started long before NASPAA came into existence. As already discussed, NASPAA's standards are designed to strongly accelerate this trend. With NASPAA now taking the lead, professionalism in public administration education may well become a reality.

Breadth of the Field

The *breadth of field* question has troubled the adherents of public administration since it first began to develop as a separate area of education. Is it public affairs, public management, city management, health management, public policy, etc.? According to NASPAA's Guidelines and Standards of 1974, it is all of them and more. The list of program specializations which are considered to be under the egis of the public administration umbrella are [18]

A. Level of Government
    1. Urban/Local
    2. State/Regional
    3. National
    4. International
B. Public Function (some examples)
    1. Community Development
    2. Criminal Justice
    3. Business Regulation
    4. Educational Administration
    5. Environmental Administration
    6. Finance and Budgeting
    7. International Development Administration
    8. Manpower and Employment
    9. National Security and Arms Control
    10. Personnel
    11. Planning
    12. Public Health
    13. Public Works Administration
    14. Transportation
    15. Urban and Regional Planning

While this is a very broad list, the notation *some examples* after *Public Function* infers that the field should not be limited to the many functions listed under B. Indeed, since 1974, health planning and administration and other nonprofit private sector activities have been receiving increasing attention in public administration programs.

Should this breadth continue to be a source of argument and concern? I think not. The formulation and the implementation of public policy are extremely broad undertakings. It would be a sad mistake to try to paint public administration into a small corner of this vast panorama. In my opinion, public administration education can effectively serve the five broad programmatic thrusts suggested by Golembiewski [19]

> *Public Affairs*, which refers to broad training for elites prepared to serve in politico/administrative roles, as diplomats or ambassadors, as high-level aids at various levels of government, etc.;
>
> *Public management*, which here refers to an emphasis on superior performance in operating jobs, especially at low to mid-managerial levels, in graduate programs having an integrative orientation;
>
> *Public management in a special locus*, such as municipal administration, city management, and so on;
>
> *Public management specialties*, which refer to personnel, planning, budgeting, and so on, which are usually concentrations or majors within an MPA program but occasionally are the prime focus for degree programs, e.g., Master in City Planning; and
>
> *Public Policy*, which refers to highly-specialized training, emphasizing mathematical and statistical tools and research designs, so as to provide powerful technical help in formulating and evaluating alternative policies and programs.

These programmatic thrusts represent both *generalist* and *specialist* approaches, with each having a significant role. They indicate the breadth of education that must be provided to properly prepare people for the variety of leadership and management positions in the public sector.

Unfortunately, though, I have to agree with Golembiewski's assertion that many PA programs tend to be conceived as a "blob" with poorly matched means–ends linkages [20]. Trying to achieve breadth by being everything to everyone has unquestionably brought weakness and discredit to the field of public administration. What can be done to eradicate the blob while at the same time retaining and strengthening the breadth and diversity of the field?

NASPAA's standards of 1977 made no attempt to narrow the program specializations previously listed from the 1974 guidelines and standards. The 1977 standards apply to all programs providing professional education for leadership and management roles in public policy and administration. Furthermore, they stress the need for flexibility and innovation in curriculum design to accommodate students with interests in a broad array of career specialty areas. Thus, NASPAA is officially promoting a very broad interpretation of the field of public administration.

But NASPAA is also attempting to improve the means–ends linkages of programs, which often have been so poorly designed. The standards address this problem in the design of program curricula by advocating a two-tier approach, wherein Tier I (Standard 4.2) consists of a set of common curriculum components expected of all students, and Tier II (Standard 4.3) consists of an array of specializations identified by each program. The development of Tier I is based on the premise that there is, indeed, a common set of knowledge and skills which are basic to both the analysis of public policy and the management of that policy in the many public sector settings.

Tier II recognizes that breadth of legitimate specialties available to programs by having each program define its objectives for advanced work and then explain how the curriculum is designed to achieve the stated objectives. The purpose of the advanced curriculum standard is to encourage all programs to design well-matched means–ends linkages into their programs, rather than to have programs consisting of an assortment of unrelated courses. Tier II should provide depth in concentration area for each student by building upon the common base in Tier I. This *building block* approach to curriculum design is standard practice in the hard sciences and professional education but is generally eschewed by liberal arts faculty.

If NASPAA is successful with the two-tier approach to curriculum design, it will mean that public administration can be defined very broadly while at the same time having strong means–ends linkages within the individual programs offered by various institutions.

A Set of Common Curriculum Components

It is generally accepted that professionalism arises from a specialized knowledge and technique acquired by extended education and training. This implies that education for public administration, to be recognized as a professional field, must embody a set of common knowledge and skills which are basic ingredients for the effective analysis and implementation of public policy. This in no way implies that all public administration programs should have a common curriculum throughout but rather acknowledges that a number of curriculum components are common to the entire breadth of public administration. If defining these components can be accomplished, then all public administration students, regardless of their areas of career interests, should be required to receive good preparation in them. If this cannot be done, as some critics maintain, then public administration is indeed a blob and does not deserve recognition as a coherent field of professional education.

The matrix of professional competencies in the 1974 guidelines and standards represents a first attempt by NASPAA to define the kinds of knowledge, skills, values, and behavior which should be characteristic of strong professional performance in making and implementing public policy. However, as indicated earlier in this chapter, the matrix is really a guide to continuing education of public managers. The all-encompassing nature of the matrix makes it ineffective as a vehicle for developing a common base of general abilities and skills for degree programs.

In 1976, the NASPAA membership approved guidelines and standards for baccalaureate degree programs [21]. These guidelines advocate a professional orientation for baccalaureate programs but emphasize the importance of a strong "arts and science foundation" at the undergraduate level. They include a chart of knowledge and skill areas, shown in Figure 1. The subject matter content of this chart was developed from the 1974 matrix of professional competencies. It contains the same five major subject areas and adds a sixth area called *arts and science foundation.* In effect, the development and approval of this chart was NASPAA's next step in defining the general abilities and skills which are common to the field of public administration. The chart provides a guide for the development of undergraduate programs in public administration and is helping to bring a more coherent focus to the field.

In 1977, as discussed in a previous section, NASPAA membership approved standards for professional master's degree programs and a peer review process to judge the substantial conformity of programs with the standards. A vital element of these standards is Standard 4.2, otherwise known as Tier I. Standard 4.2 is hopefully another step forward in defining the basic multidisciplinary underpinnings of public administration. These common curriculum components represent a compromise that the NASPAA Standards Committee was able to reach in 1977. Refinements will undoubtedly be made in future years as NASPAA attempts to apply the standards in the peer review process.

Standard 4.2 actually consists of two major sections [16]:

4.21 A demonstrated ability (implies competency) to:
   —define and diagnose decision situations, collect relevant data, perform logical analysis, develop alternatives, implement a course of action, and evaluate results;
   —organize and communicate clearly to a variety of audiences

CHART OF KNOWLEDGE AND SKILL AREAS FOR BACCALAUREATE DEGREES IN PUBLIC AFFAIRS/PUBLIC ADMINISTRATION

Major Subject Areas	Recommended Ordering of Topics from Freshman through Senior Year
	Freshman Year . . . . Senior Year
-A- Political Social Economics Legal	(. . . Government institutions, powers, relationships . . .) (. . . Cultural and social mores and patterns; ethical behavior and issues . . .) (. . . Legislative processes) (. . . Political theory and values.) (. . . Social and environmental issues) (. . . Micro and macro economic analysis . . .) (. . . Legal institutions and processes . . .)
-B- Analytical Tools: Quant & Non-quant	(Algebra, finite mathematics and basic concepts of calculus) (. . . Probability and statistics.) (. . . Intro to electronic data processing) (. . . Basic accounting systems) (. . . Oral and written communication skills) (. . . Applications of computers and quantitative tools. . .)
-C- Individual Group Organization Dynamics	(Organization structure, processes and dynamics) (Individual motivation, dynamics of groups, modes of leadership) (. . . Psychology) (. . . Sociology)
-D- Policy Analysis	(Formulating and evaluating public policy (cost-benefit, social impact) (Application of knowledge and skill areas to public issues and problems)
-E- Administrative/ management processes	(Budgeting and financial management) (Program planning and operations management) (Personnel administration and labor relations) (Application of analytical and behavior tools to management and organizational problems.)
-F- Arts and Science Foundation	(. . . Natural sciences, social sciences, and humanities. . .) (in addition to subject matter already included in A, B, and C above)

Figure 1   Knowledge and skill areas for baccalaureate degrees. (From Ref. 21.)

through formats including verbal presentations, written memorandum and technical reports, and statistical charts, graphs, and tables.

4.22 A basic understanding and ability (implies a good exposure to the subject) to deal with:
—the cultural, ethical, and social values important to democratic society, constitutionalism, and the rule of law;
—the political processes that influence the formulation and implementation of public policy;
—the levels and institutions of government, including their power and relationships;
—the economic and legal environment as it affects both the public and private sectors;
—organizations and management concepts;
—individual, group, and intergroup behavior, motivation, leadership, and communications;
—administrative planning and control systems;
—the application of quantitative and economic tools and decision models;
—introductory explanatory data and statistical analysis procedures, electronic data processing, and the use of statistical packages;
—introductory accounting, budgeting and financial management systems;
—personnel management and labor relations systems.

Standard 4.21 stipulates that programs should stress the development of competencies in decision making and communications throughout the curriculum. These competencies are considered to be absolutely essential to effective policy analysis and management of public programs.

First, Standard 4.21 calls for the development of a student's analytical abilities for problem solving and decision making, as opposed to the more traditional descriptive and library research approaches of the liberal arts. This involves a change in learning materials, teaching methods, and educational philosophy. While readings and library research still should play an important part, strong emphasis must be placed on decision-oriented cases, simulation exercises, field activities including internships, and applied empirical research. All successful fields of professional education include a heavy "hands-on" component to bridge the gap between academic theory and applied reality.

Second, Standard 4.21 stresses that all public administration professionals should be able to effectively organize information and communicate it clearly, both in written form and orally, to a variety of audiences. The development of good writing and speaking skills is a particularly weak aspect of American education in general and public administration education in particular. Analytical skills and encyclopedic knowledge are of greatly diminished value if the results of applying the knowledge and skills cannot be effectively communicated.

Standard 4.22 contains areas of knowledge and skills which are believed to be common to the entire breadth of the field and thus desirable for all individuals who practice public administration. The areas are not intended to prescribe specific courses, even though the development of basic skills in some of them may be done most efficiently in that way. Some of the areas, involving mainly descriptions of processes and institutions, may be handled best through integration with other topics. For example, the study of cultural, ethical, and social values and political processes may be strengthened by their integration into relevant courses throughout a program's core requirements and elective areas. On the other hand, development of basic skills in statistics, computer analysis, and economic analysis is probably most efficiently done by separate required courses.

In the application of 4.22, it must also be recognized that different levels of the quantitative skill areas are essential for students interested in generalist management positions as contrasted to those desiring to enter policy and program analysis, operations analysis, or the design of information systems. All students need to become intelligent consumers and evaluators of studies involving economic and quantitative analysis. They need to understand the nature of assumptions made and the limitations of methods used concerning the problem at hand. They also must be able to intelligently interpret and understand the meaning of the results in order for the results to be used appropriately in decision making. This kind of understanding can be gained only through a very applied approach to the teaching of the quantitative areas. In addition to this "intelligent consumer" level of understanding, students desiring a career in policy or operations analysis need a more in-depth understanding of the various quantitative tools available. The latter need can be developed in the elective or specialty areas for individual students.

There is no doubt in the author's mind that, as of 1981, most public administration programs are not in substantial conformance with the spirit and purpose of Standards 4.21 and 4.22. However, the self-study reports submitted for the first round of peer review indicate that these standards are causing considerable self-evaluation and redesign of curricula throughout the country. It appears that the common curriculum component standards will make a substantial impact on defining and strengthening the field.

Advanced Work or Specialty Areas

Standard 4.2 is intended to be a common springboard for launching into advanced graduate work of a generalist or specialty nature. The advanced work in a program is covered by Standard 4.3, otherwise known as Tier II. The standard reads as follows [16]:

> 4.3 *Advanced Curriculum Components.* For advanced work beyond the common curriculum components, programs have considerable latitude in shaping their curricula to achieve their objectives. Each program shall clearly define its objectives for advanced work, the rationale for the objectives, and explanation of how the curriculum is designed to achieve those objectives. The statement of objectives shall include any program specializations and the main categories of students to be served (pre-service, in-service, full-time, part-time, etc.). The explanation should indicate how the curriculum relates to the unique environmental conditions for the selected specialty fields. It should also include the application of analytical tools to policy and management decision situations, and advanced work in administrative/management processes.
>
> If a program offers specialty fields, those fields shall comply fully with the Standards, i.e., the specialty should be incorporated into a masters program in PA. The specialty shall not be a substitute for the Common Curriculum Components in Section 4.2. If a program advertises its ability to provide preparation for a specialty field in its catalog, bulletin, brochures, and/or posters, evidence shall be given that key courses in the specialty are offered on a regular basis by faculty qualified in the specialty. Specialty courses may be courses other than those offered directly by the PA unit.

This standard stresses the need for clear objectives and a rational means–ends linkage for any advanced work or specialty offered by a program. It does not specify what kinds of specialties are appropriate or what content they should contain. But it does place the onus for rational program design directly on the program's faculty. It is believed that this approach to advanced curriculum design will allow flexibility and creativity to flourish while at the same time requiring strong means–ends linkages within programs.

In supporting Standard 4.3, NASPAA has chosen to define public administration as a field with a very broad spectrum. Actually, there was probably no other choice, as any narrow definition would most likely be unacceptable to a majority of the academics and practitioners in the field.

Conclusions

Since 1974, NASPAA has been engaged in a continuing effort to define and improve the field of public administration. The most visible impacts of this effort on the field are likely to be (1) broad acceptance of public administration as a field of multidisciplinary professional education; (2) recognition that a very broad array of public functions or specialties under the public administration umbrella can be a strength, rather than a weakness, if program design is handled properly; (3) eventual acceptance of a set of general knowledge, abilities, and skills as a common base for all programs; and (4) program designs which provide strong means–ends linkages between the common core of knowledge and skills and advanced work.

With regard to the eventual success of NASPAA's efforts, I agree with Waldo [22]:

> I see a strengthened center in NASPAA, especially in those programs that seek to provide a professional-type education—programs that are interdisciplinary and are at once demanding with respect to a required core curriculum, and permissive with respect to specialization and experimentation. I expect this strengthened center not only to survive but to increase in size, influence, and acceptability.

References

1. NASPAA was formed in 1970 as an affiliate of the American Society for Public Administration. As of 1980, NASPAA membership included undergraduate and graduate programs at over 220 colleges and universities.
2. Dwight Waldo, "Introduction: Trends and Issues in Education for Public Administration," in Guthrie S. Birkhead and James D. Carroll (eds.), *Education for Public Service 1979*, Maxwell School, Syracuse University, Utica, N.Y., 1979, pp. 16–17.
3. For example, see Dwight Waldo, *The Enterprise of Public Administration*, Chandler & Sharp, Novato, Calif., 1980; Guthrie S. Birkhead and James D. Carroll (eds.), *Education for Public Service 1979*, Maxwell School, Syracuse University, Utica, N.Y., 1979; Frederick C.

Mosher (ed.), *American Public Administration: Past, Present, Future,* University of Alabama Press, University, Ala., 1975; Richard L. Chapman and Frederick N. Cleaveland, *Meeting the Needs of Tomorrow's Public Service: Guidelines for Professional Education in Public Administration,* The National Academy of Public Administration, Washington, D.C., 1973.

4. *Guidelines and Standards for Professional Master's Degree Programs in Public Affairs/Public Administration,* National Association of Schools of Public Affairs and Administration, Washington, D.C., 1974.

5. Richard L. Chapman and Frederick N. Cleaveland, *Meeting the Needs of Tomorrow's Public Service: Guidelines for Professional Education in Public Administration,* The National Academy of Public Administration, Washington, D.C., 1973, p. 53.

6. *Guidelines and Standards,* NASPAA, 1974, pp. 29–33.

7. *Guidelines and Standards,* NASPAA, 1974, pp. 7–12.

8. As chairperson of the NASPAA Standards Committee from 1976–1978, the author participated in this review process and in the development of the 1977 NASPAA standards.

9. Alice B. Stone and Donald C. Stone, "Early Development of Education in Public Administration," in Frederick C. Mosher (ed.), *American Public Administration: Past, Present, Future,* University of Alabama Press, University, Ala., 1975, p. 26.

10. Don K. Price, *The Scientific Estate,* Harvard University Press, Cambridge, Mass., 1965, pp. 120–269.

11. Richard L. Schott, "Public Administration as a Profession: Problems and Prospects," *Public Administration Review,* 36(3) (May/June 1976):253–259.

12. Dwight Waldo, "Scope of the Theory of Public Administration," in *Theory and Practice of Public Administration: Scope, Objectives, and Methods,* The American Academy of Political and Social Science, Philadelphia, 1968; Dwight Waldo, "Education for Public Administration in the Seventies," in Frederick C. Mosher (ed.), *American Public Administration: Past, Present, Future,* University of Alabama Press, University, Ala., 1975, pp. 222–226; H. George Frederickson, "Public Administration in the 1970's: Developments and Directions," *Public Administration Review,* 36(5) (September/October 1976):574–576.

13. Dwight Waldo, "Scope of the Theory of Public Administration," in *Theory and Practice of Public Administration: Scope Objectives and*

Methods, The American Academy of Political and Social Science, Philadelphia, 1968, p. 40.

14. Allen Schick, "The Trauma of Politics: Public Administration in the Sixties," in Frederick C. Mosher (ed.), *American Public Administration: Past, Present, Future,* University of Alabama Press, University, Ala., 1975, p. 159.

15. Richard L. Schott, "Public Administration as a Profession: Problems and Prospects," *Public Administration Review,* 36(3) (September/October 1976):253–258.

16. The Standards for Professional Master's Degree Programs in Public Affairs and Administration were issued on mimeographed sheets by the National Association of Schools of Public Affairs and Administration in November 1977.

17. Guthrie S. Birkhead, "Standards and Educational Institutions," *The Bureaucrat,* 6(2) (Summer 1977):25.

18. *Guidelines and Standards,* NASPAA, 1974, pp. 12–13.

19. Robert T. Golembiewski, "The Near-Future of Graduate Public Administration Programs in the U.S.," *Southern Review of Public Administration,* 3(3) (December 1979):343.

20. Robert T. Golembiewski, "The Near-Future of Graduate Public Administration Programs in the U.S.," *Southern Review of Public Administration,* 3(3) (December 1979):342–343.

21. *Guidelines and Standards for Baccalaureate Degree Programs in Public Affairs/Public Administration,* National Association of Schools of Public Affairs and Administration, Washington, D.C., 1976, pp. 6–9.

22. Dwight Waldo, "Introduction: Trends and Issues in Education for Public Administration," in Guthrie S. Birkhead and James D. Carroll (eds.), *Education for Public Service 1979,* Maxwell School, Syracuse University, Utica, N.Y., 1979, pp. 23–24.

Part 2

Prominent Persons in Public Administration

All too often academic and professional publications pursue research and educational objectives to the exclusion of insights into the lives and works of the significant persons to whom the subject matter under discussion owes a great debt. In this inaugural issue of the *Annals of Public Administration,* we initiate a section that seeks to highlight and analyze in a brief, yet substantive, manner the contributions of several scholars to the history and theory of public administration.

No effort is made herein to suggest any heirarchy of prominent contributors to the field of public administration. Not that any of the three persons included—Dwight Waldo, Herbert Simon, and Harold Lasswell— would not fit into such a listing; each could have been so highlighted.

The initial selections, a decision of the topic-area editor, were intended to provide a broad range of contributions to the field and to fully use the talents of scholars in public administration already doing research in the traditions of the persons honored in this section. As future publications in this topic area are developed, so also will the contributions of other persons be presented and discussed.

5

Dwight Waldo

Laurence J. O'Toole, Jr.
Auburn University, Auburn, Alabama

In this chapter some of Dwight Waldo's contributions to the history and theory of public administration are briefly summarized. His efforts as political theorist, administrative historian, chronicler of the field, and stimulant of new ideas have been highly significant.

Probably no individual has been more intimately connected with the subject of this volume, public administration history and theory, than Dwight Waldo. He has filled several unique roles, to be sketched below, in the field of public administration; and in this process he has helped to enlarge considerably the pool of knowledge which the modern world possesses about its administrative activities.

Waldo has been a scholar of public administration in its broadest sense. This observation may seem like a contradiction in terms, since to many observers public administration epitomizes narrow technicism. Not so for Waldo, however. Throughout his career he has remained interested not only in virtually every facet of administrative activity and learning but also in the larger features of the social world which shape and are themselves formed by the administrative centers of the world's many governments.

Waldo's contributions to public administration have been manifold. He himself served as a federal bureaucrat during World War II in two organizations (the Office of Price Administration and the Bureau of the Budget) then heavily populated with academics interested in public administration. He directed a university bureau of public service research for a decade. He educated large numbers of future public administrators and professors of the subject during his several decades at Berkeley and Syracuse. He recently completed a term of service as President of the National Association of Schools of Public Affairs and Administration. But it is his scholarship, his written contribution to the corpus of administrative thought, which is perhaps his most significant and lasting achievement. Waldo's published work is thus the major subject of discussion here.

Throughout Dwight Waldo's nearly four decades as a scholar he has kept busy at research and writing. Waldo always has tackled questions of major significance, and he has written only when he has had something to say. Nevertheless, in terms not only of quality but also of quantity, his product has been consistently impressive. He has authored or edited more than 60 published items, including 11 books and monographs. His contributions have been tremendously varied in scope and intent, so that even a catalog, let alone an analysis, of his efforts must lie beyond the scope of this brief chapter. Instead, I have chosen to review briefly some of the intellectual roles he has occupied in the course of his productive career.

Waldo as Political Theorist

If there has been one important question which has occupied Dwight Waldo's thought throughout his entire career, that question would probably be the following: What problems and opportunities does administration in idea and practice pose for democracy and vice versa? This fundamental question of political philosophy lurked behind Waldo's initial foray into the field in his doctoral dissertation and even now animates him—he currently labors on a book-length treatment of the problem. In this role, perhaps more clearly than elsewhere, is visible one of Waldo's rarest characteristics, his capacity to be simultaneously scientist and humanist.

His talent is evident in *The Administrative State* [1], the published version of his dissertation research. Although one of his earliest contributions to the field, this volume remains one of Waldo's most important efforts. (In fact, if one relies upon the *Social Sciences Citation Index* as a measure of scholarly influence, *The Administrative State*, now 33 years after publication, still ranks as his premier product.)

The Administrative State was, as its subtitle stated, a definitive "Study of the Political Theory of American Public Administration." As such, it was and remains unique in scope, comprehensiveness, and insight. Scholarly contemporaries of his such as Herbert Simon, Norton Long, Wallace Sayre, and others were to match Waldo in critique of both the simplistic "administrative dogmas" (to borrow Francis Coker's phrase) earlier in vogue and also the lack of attention given to the intermixture of politics and administration. But Waldo alone brought the training and sensitivities of the political theorist to his analysis of administrative ideas. In that study, and frequently since then, he searched through American administrative thought to expose and criticize its premises and conclusions. His technique has been to pose to public administration the timeless questions discussed by political philosophers throughout the ages: Who should rule? Why? What are the aims of government? And so forth. By demonstrating conclusively that "orthodox" American public administrative thought was itself a political theory, and by raising serious questions about possible inconsistencies between it and democratic government, Waldo helped influence American administrative ideas in at least two significant respects. First, his work helped demolish the consensus which had existed about the supposedly enduring value of the early administrative principles. Waldo assisted in the destruction of the oversimplified doctrines that earlier had united administrative reformers. And second, by continuing over the years to apply the perspective of the political theorist to the various changes in administrative fashion—whether systems theory, development administration, or the "new public administration"—he has made those who engage in public administration as an intellectual activity more aware of their own values and antecedents, less prone to hubris over their intellectual achievements or supposed political neutrality. Public administrators have been richer for Waldo's constant and well-defended reminder that they deal in important questions of governance and that both the timeworn and newfangled trappings of bureaucracy may bear upon the likelihood of free and just government.

In a way it is surprising that this significant contribution of Waldo, his service as political theorist for the field and profession, is so highly valued today by his colleagues. Immediate reaction to *The Administrative State* by the public administration community had been negative. An early evaluation of Waldo's first book in the *Public Administration Review* was harsh. And for the next several years of his career, Waldo was relatively unwelcome among public administrationists (see, e.g., Ref. 2, p. 7), perhaps because he had alienated that group by his trenchant analysis of its dominant beliefs. Yet the strength and value of his work gradually won adherents there and elsewhere. And although Waldo has added plenty to his written work on public administration, *The Administrative State* itself has remained in print throughout his long career. Everywhere, serious students of the field are indebted to this analysis.

Other Roles

If Dwight Waldo had busied himself only with the political theory of American public administration, his contribution would have been substantial. But while he is perhaps best known for being public administration's distinguished political-theorist-in-residence, other interests have often captured his attention. Through these additional scholarly concerns, he has even more significantly affected the study and practice of administrative life.

Waldo as Administrative Historian

One interest has been the realm of administrative history. Throughout his professional career Waldo has been concerned with how, when, and why various administrative ideas, apparatuses, and innovations developed. His view has been that one must look to the past—indeed sometimes the distant past—to gain a proper understanding of the present.

Clearly, for instance, one of the social scientists ultimately most influential on Waldo's thinking was Max Weber, whom Waldo has studied and referenced for decades. Waldo shares with Weber not only detailed interest in the many strengths and weaknesses of bureaucracy as a form of social organization but also a curiosity about administrative arrangements spanning cultures and millennia. Why has administrative advance occurred as it has? What has been the role of the state in fostering or shaping it? Under what conditions does the Western liberal idea of public bureaucracy thrive? What alternative versions have been possible? Questions such as these have interested both men. While Weber was much more the original scholar on this terrain, Waldo has continually reminded administrative thinkers of the importance of these issues. His most recent volume, *The Enterprise of Public Administration* [3], has as a major theme the importance of the historical roots of modern public administration—such as the connection between the rise of civilization and the development of administration and the significance for modern times of the administrative arrangements in ancient Rome. As a historian, especially an intellectual historian of the field, therefore, Waldo has provided further rare enlightenment.

Waldo as Chronicler

In a rough combination of his roles as political theorist and historian, Dwight Waldo has often taken on the burden of recording in print the continuing developments in the field of public administration. Throughout the past quarter-century, whenever shifts in intellectual interest, academic emphasis, or research subjects have occurred in the public administration community, Waldo has observed these, sought to render them understandable to those in many subspecialties, and suggested what other shifts might be forthcoming. In this respect he has performed a unique service for administrative thinkers by allowing many people, fragmented by diverse interests, some understanding of developments across the whole subject of public administration. Through one or another published product (see, e.g., Refs. 4, 5, 6, 7, 8, 9, and 10) Waldo has almost single-handedly integrated large portions of seemingly diverse public administration thought. There may be no one who surveys the field so widely or treats its intellectual products so seriously, albeit not without a touch of humor when appropriate. In this role, too, he has been without peer.

Waldo as Stimulant

If Waldo began his career as an "external" critic of the American public administration movement, nevertheless even at the outset his criticism was softened by sympathy with and respect for the ideas of that movement. As he put it, he "came to have a basic respect for the achievement, for the product [i.e., public administration thought], *considered as a political theory*" (see Ref. 2, p. 6, emphasis in original). And even *The Administrative State* suggested Waldo's basic agreement with some of the broad goals of the early reform efforts. Since that time, he has endeavored to facilitate the advancement and communication of significant administrative ideas developed by others.

He served in this capacity as Director of Berkeley's Institute of Governmental Studies and as Editor-in-Chief of the *Public Administration Review* for 11 years. Perhaps the best examples of Waldo's service as stimulant to the public administration community came during his years at the Maxwell School of Syracuse University. Waldo was appointed as Syracuse's first Albert Schweitzer Professor in the Humanities in 1967. Over the succeeding years he utilized the state funding provided with the chaired position to enable new, promising, and significant ideas about public administration to be heard and published. For instance, his generosity was responsible for the convening of the Minnowbrook Conference in 1968 which signaled the rise of the new public administration. The ideas of that group of young thinkers were published and received wide attention [11]. Waldo helped to underwrite another volume, written mostly by others, on similar themes [12]. And he funded a conference of distinguished theorists on "Organizations for the Future" (see, e.g., Ref. 13).

These instances by no means complete the list of Waldo's contributions in this regard. But they serve as samples of his considerable efforts and scholarly convictions. Waldo frequently labored to bring attention to ideas which he himself seriously questioned. For instance, he has hardly been an ardent advocate of many of the nostrums of the new public administration. He has sometimes served as devil's advocate against positions he helped sponsor or facilitate. Always the intellectual liberal, however, he has acted on the presumption that all are served if ideas are freely and easily exchanged, if established perspectives are occasionally looked at afresh. By virtue of the beliefs and contributions of this individual, public administration thought is more plural and less respectful of mere convention than it otherwise would have been.

Conclusion

I have touched upon some aspects of Dwight Waldo's numerous contributions to public administration. However, space does not permit discussion of many other of his scholarly strengths. For instance, it has not been possible to say much about his important research in subspecialties such as the theory of organization or comparative and development administration. Nor can one even begin to convey a sense of his more personal contributions to students and colleagues who, in search of enlightenment or encouragement, have tapped his seemingly bottomless reservoir of insight, grace, and good humor. In more respects than it is possible to suggest, he has brought erudition to his profession and nobility to his calling.

References

1. Dwight Waldo, *The Administrative State: A Study of the Political Theory of American Public Administration*, Ronald, New York, 1948.
2. Dwight Waldo, "The Administrative State Revisited," *Public Administration Review*, 25 (March 1965):5–30.
3. Dwight Waldo, *The Enterprise of Public Administration*, Chandler & Sharp, Novato, Calif., 1980.

4. Dwight Waldo, *The Study of Public Administration*, Doubleday, New York, 1955.
5. Dwight Waldo, Comments on "Research on Government, Politics, and Administration," in *Research for Public Policy*, Brookings Dedication Lectures, Brookings, Washington, D.C., 1961, pp. 21–29.
6. Dwight Waldo, "Public Administration," in *International Encyclopedia of the Social Sciences*, vol. 13, Macmillan and Free Press, New York, 1968, pp. 145–146.
7. Dwight Waldo, "Public Administration," *Journal of Politics*, 30 (May 1968):443–479.
8. Dwight Waldo, "Public Administration in a Time of Revolutions," *Public Administration Review*, 28 (July/August 1968):362–368.
9. Dwight Waldo, "Developments in Public Administration," *The Annals*, 404 (November 1972):217–254.
10. Dwight Waldo, "Education for Public Administration in the Seventies," in Frederick C. Mosher (ed.), *American Public Administration: Past, Present, Future*, University of Alabama Press, University, Ala., 1975, pp. 181–232.
11. Frank Marini (ed.), *Toward a New Public Administration: The Minnowbrook Perspective*, Chandler, Scranton, Pa., 1971.
12. Dwight Waldo (ed.), *Public Administration in a Time of Turbulence*, Chandler, Scranton, Pa., 1971.
13. Dwight Waldo (ed.), "Organizations for the Future," *Public Administration Review*, 33 (July/August 1973):299–335.

6

Herbert Simon: Contributions and Controversies

Luther F. Carter
College of Charleston, Charleston, South Carolina

Buford L. Brinlee
University of North Florida, Jacksonville, Florida

The impact of Herbert Simon on the development of public administration theory spans several decades. This overview emphasizes those major contributions which Simon is associated with and suggests that although his influence loomed large upon the field for a short time, his empiricism precluded an even greater significance for the development of more useful approaches to public policy and decision making in the public sector.

Introduction

To review the work of any productive scholar over a 30-year period is an ambitious task. When the subject is Herbert Simon, one of the most prolific and respected social scientists in recent history, the task is especially difficult. Not everyone, after all, wins the Nobel prize.

From the perspective of public administration, two characteristics emerge from Simon's work that perhaps best summarize his relationship to the discipline. The first is the apparent shift in his research orientation from the broader concern with administrative behavior expressed in his work in the late 1940s to the more specific focus on decision theory evident two decades later. The other interesting facet of Simon's career has been his proclivity to challenge some of the premiere names in the social sciences along the way. The thesis of this review is that both characteristics reflect the underlying continuity in his theoretical orientation as a logical

115

positivist, an orientation which has continued into his later career, as evidenced by his increasing infatuation with computer technology. Decision theory has consistently been the rubric which facilitates the "interface" between his philosophical and mechanistic view of the world.

Theoretical Challenges and Personal Disagreements

The publication of *Administrative Behavior* [1] marked Simon's emergence as an acknowledged authority in public administration. As the angry young man, he attacked the traditional canons of administration, provided a clearer articulation of the fact–value dichotomy, and developed an analytical view of organizations previously lacking in the literature. In the process, Simon directly confronted the principles of Luther Gulick and the entire departmentalist school. The strength of his arguments stemmed from two distinct yet related approaches. First, he undermined the validity of the departmentalist argument on its own terms by pointing out internal inconsistencies. His assertion that the "scientific principles" were no more than "proverbs" was based on simple, logical reasoning. Second, having undercut the theoretical foundation of this existing paradigm, he proceeded to construct a revised theory of administration from the behavioralist perspective. The success of Simon's new paradigm was indicated by the acceptance of administrative behavior as the prevailing focus during the next decade. To this day, *Administrative Behavior* remains one of the true classics in public administration.

Having set forth this seminal merging of logical rigor and the behavioral perspective, Simon insisted on similar standards throughout the discipline, standards that functionally required the separation of facts from value. The extent to which this analytical distinction was applicable to public administration or other areas of political inquiry soon became a major issue of contention. An excellent example of Simon's attempt at enforcing his rigorous standards is apparent in the disagreement with Dwight Waldo's "Development of Theory of Democratic Administration" in 1952 [2]. Waldo maintained that the fact–value dichotomy was inapplicable in public administration theory and raised serious questions about an approach which denied normative considerations.

In an acerbic exchange, Simon took Waldo and other political theorists to task, asserting that they "continue to think and write in the loose literary, metaphorical style." Furthermore, he challenged their reasoning by maintaining that "the standard of rigor that is tolerated in political theory would not receive a passing grade in the elementary course in logic, Aristotelian or symbolic." In contrast, Simon stressed his own cautious approach (Ref. 2, p. 494):

> Study of logic and empirical science has impressed on me the extreme care that must be exercised, in the search for truth, to avoid logical booby traps.

Waldo responded as follows (Ref. 3, p. 501):

> Professor Simon seems to me that rare individual in our secular age, a man of deep faith. His convictions are monolithic and massive. His toleration of heresy and sin is nil. The Road to Salvation is straight, narrow, one-way, and privately owned.

Given this level of discourse, it is not surprising that Simon subsequently shifted his orientation to organizations in general, decision making in particular, and the broader audience which would appreciate his contributions [4].

His work increasingly emphasized the generic organization and specifically the decision-making processes associated with this social structure. Thus the coauthor of the text *Public Administration* in 1950 [5] became the coauthor of *Organizations* in 1957 [6]. *Organizations* represents the authors' quest to discover and catalog the characteristics of organizations sui generis.

Their behavioral model of the organization reflects a complex, goal-oriented system which mediates the needs of its employees and its external environment. Organizational behavior at the individual unit and organizational levels consists of "bounded rationality" which results from limitations inherent in the cognitive processes of the individual (satisficing rather than maximizing), the conflicting needs of the various units within the organization itself, and the constraints of its external environment. To handle the vast array of variables required for this model, ranging from psychologically based individual cognitive processes to environmental conditions, the authors employ a biological metaphor. That is, " . . . the general picture of the human organism that [they] use to analyze organization behavior . . . is a picture of a choosing, decision-making, problem-solving organism . . . " (Ref. 6, p. 11).

Difficulties are encountered, however, when this metaphor is applied to social science phenomena. Specifically, how can the interrelationship between the various component parts of the organization (individual, group, and total) be operationalized to explain their relative importance in the organization's behavior, either at a single point in time or over a longer period? This entails the notorious unit of analysis problem, an issue that

public choice theorists have struggled with in vain for the past two decades, as represented by their inability to resolve the dilemma over the interpersonal comparison of utility [7].

While public administration theorists have been prone to avoid this
seemingly unresolvable aspect of the decision-making process, preferring
instead to emphasize the political nature of public organizations, Simon
has not only followed the imperatives of his logical and empirical orientation but also attempted to resolve the specification problems attendent this
perspective [8]. In retrospect, the marginal importance of Simon's post-
Organizations work to public administration reflects an internal con-
sistency in his own philosophical position as to how social phenomena
should be studied [9].

The importance of the decision-making process in organizations has
been recognized by a variety of scholars in studying both private and
public organizations. Private sector applications have focused on the
behavior of the firm [10] and especially on the acquisition of computer
equipment [11,12]. In the public sector, studies range from municipal and
state budgeting behavior [13,14] to decisions made by federal field offices
in a state [15] and by national leaders during international crises [16]. The
decision-making paradigm has also been adopted for a number of case
studies in the growing field of policy analysis. As Theodore Lowi [17] has
noted, however, this marriage between decision making and policy making has been accomplished at the expense of blurring the individual identi-
ties of both partners.

Simon's obsession with the decision process continues through *The
New Science of Management Decision* [18], *The Shape of Automation*
[19], and *The New Science of Management Decision*, 3d ed. [20]. In these
later works, his repeated attempts to develop a single model based on individual thought processes require a hierarchy of organizational control
such that internal conflict can be resolved and hence the interpersonal
comparison of utility dilemma obviated. As noted earlier in *Organizations*
(Ref. 6, p. 127):

> The greater the number of independent information sources, the greater
> the differentiation of perceptions within the organization. Thus, we
> would expect less perceptual conflict in an organization where one out-
> side individual or group of individuals holds an acknowledged monop-
> oly of relevant information than where there are a number of external
> sources.

The necessity for such control is clearly indicated in the latest edition of
The New Science of Management Decision through his description of the

organization as a three-layered structure with a nonprogrammed decision structure at the top which effectively designs and controls the programmed decision below (Ref. 20, pp. 110–113). The technological system requires a monopoly on information (the basic unit of all "factual" decisions) which is antithetical to the humanist call for greater individual responsibility and participation in the decision-making process. Control, of information *and* decisions *and* ultimately behavior, is critical to the success of the organization.

The hierarchical implications of Simon's decision-making model and its control over individuals in organizations was a point of contention in his disagreement with Argyris in 1973 [21]. In continuing to refute the humanist call for greater individual freedom in organizations, Simon maintains that "the desire to destroy authority relations often conceals the desire to replace them with one's own authority" (see Ref. 20, p. 99). Here again we see Simon's consistent attempt to achieve a fact–value separation and the degree of relativity which logically ensues. Over two decades earlier he maintained "that definitions which equate influence or power with the values an individual possesses are unsuitable for political science" (see Ref. 22, p. 501). To the earlier humanists and the current advocates of the new public administration, such a separation is logically impossible. Indeed, the relationship among power, authority, and values is not only critical to an understanding of administrative behavior but also to the implementation of public policy in a democratic society.

Conclusion

We find it interesting that a career launched on a criticism of the departmentalists should result in such a heavy reliance on organizational structure, having replaced their earlier "principles" with decision rules which have similarly rigid implications for the people who work in organizations. Rules, be they "principles" or "decisions," control administrative behavior.

Simon's work has had a multiplier effect in a number of social science areas. The discipline of public administration, in particular, may have been better served had Simon pursued his vigorous empiricism in questions of public policy and governmental decision making rather than devoting his attention to the generic organization. However, his later contributions have not been a complete loss to the discipline; only their applicability to the public sector remains doubtful. Unable to resolve the somewhat fuzzy requirements of a democratic state, Simon's work manifests the policy–administration dichotomy demarcated by Woodrow Wilson almost a century earlier.

References

1. Herbert A. Simon, *Administrative Behavior: A Study of Decision-Making Processes in Administrative Organization*, Free Press, New York, 1947.
2. Herbert A. Simon, " 'Development of Theory of Democratic Administration': Replies and Comments," *American Politcal Science Review*, 46 (1952):494–496.
3. Dwight Waldo, " 'Development of Theory of Democratic Administration': Replies and Comments," *American Political Science Review*, 46 (1952):500–503.
4. Herbert A. Simon, "Comments on the Theory of Organization," *The American Political Science Review*, 46 (April 1952):1130–1139.
5. Herbert A. Simon, Donald W. Smithburg, and Victor A. Thompson, *Public Administration*, Knopf, New York, 1950.
6. James G. March and Herbert A. Simon, *Organizations*, Wiley, New York, 1957.
7. See William H. Riker and Peter C. Ordeshook, *An Introduction to Positive Political Theory*, Prentice-Hall, Englewood Cliffs, N.J., 1973, pp. 21–23.
8. Herbert A. Simon, "Causal Ordering and Identifiability," in Tjalling Koopmans (ed.), *Econometric Methods*, Cowles Commission for Research in Economics Monograph No. 14, Wiley, New York, 1953.
9. For a discussion of this controversy over method, see Herbert J. Storing, "The Science of Administration: Herbert Simon," in Herbert J. Storing (ed.), *Essays on the Scientific Study of Politics*, Holt, Rinehart and Winston, New York, 1962.
10. Richard M. Cyert and James G. March, *A Behavioral Theory of the Firm*, Prentice-Hall, Englewood Cliffs, N.J., 1963.
11. Eugene E. Carter, "Project Evaluations and Firm Decisions," *The Journal of Management Studies*, 8 (October 1971):253–379.
12. Eugene E. Carter, "The Behavioral Theory of the Firm and Top Level Corporate Decisions," *Administrative Sciences Quarterly*, 16 (December 1971):413–428.
13. John P. Crecine, *Government Problem Solving: A Computer Simulation of Municipal Budgeting*, Rand McNally, Skokie, Ill., 1968.
14. Rufus P. Browning, "Innovative and Noninnovative Decision Processes in Government Budgeting," in Ira Sharkansky (ed.), *Policy Analysis in Political Science*, Markham, Chicago, 1970, pp. 304–334.
15. William J. Gore, "Administrative Decision Making in Federal Field

Offices," *Public Administration Review*, 16 (Autumn 1956):287–291.

16. Graham T. Allison, "Conceptual Models and the Cuban Missile Crisis," *The American Political Science Review*, 63 (September 1969): 689–718.
17. Theodore Lowi, "Decision Making vs. Policy Making: Toward an Antidote for Technocracy," *Public Administration Review*, 30 (May/June 1970):314–325.
18. Herbert A. Simon, *The New Science of Management Decision*, 1st ed., Harper & Row, New York, 1965.
19. Herbert A. Simon, *The Shape of Automation for Men and Management*, Harper & Row, New York, 1965.
20. Herbert A. Simon, *The New Science of Management Decision*, 3rd ed., Prentice-Hall, Englewood Cliffs, N.J., 1977.
21. The Chris Argyris and Herbert Simon exchanges are contained throughout *Public Administration Review*, 33 (1973).
22. Herbert A. Simon, "Notes on the Observation and Measurement of Political Power," *The Journal of Politics*, 15 (November 1953):501.

7

Harold Lasswell's Contribution to Public Administration: An Overview

Miriam Ershkowitz
Temple University, Philadelphia, Pennsylvania

This brief overview of Harold Lasswell's contribution to public administration is designed to highlight a number of conceptual areas in which Lasswell pioneered with theoretical explanations of organizational phenomena. In addition, Lasswell's strong personal interest in the teaching and practice of public administration is reviewed.

Introduction

In this brief chapter, the role of Harold D. Lasswell in shaping contemporary public administration theory and practice will be examined. Lasswell was a prolific writer whose work was characterized by sophisticated conceptualizations of important ideas in a language he literally invented. He was an exemplary public administrator himself, serving as an advisor to state and local governments and to several American presidents, commencing with Franklin Roosevelt. He was an active participant in the organization of numerous national and international public organizations [1].

In addition, just as he trained thousands of lawyers from all parts of the globe while at Yale, so did he provide similar academic and professional training for hundreds of public administrators at several Eastern academic institutions in the many years after his retirement from Yale. Lasswell prepared intricate plans for training administrators, analyzing the value orientations of the sociopolitical process; conceived innovative structures of decision making; and produced seminal early work on the psychology of organizational leadership. This review of Lasswell's contributions is designed to serve as a stimulus for other analyses of Lasswell's work by students concerned about the intellectual heritage of public administration.

Lasswell's Life and Work

Harold D. Lasswell, who died in December 1978 at the age of 76, is widely hailed as the leading social scientist in the United States in the twentieth century. After constructing theories on the psychosocial aspects of political behavior and the importance of empiricism in social science, Lasswell went on to create the concept of policy sciences and wrote extensively on this topic as well as on decision making and other topics central to public management. He established the Policy Science Center in New York City and trained several generations of policy scientists at Yale, John Jay, Temple, and other noted universities throughout the world. His 50 major works have been translated into many languages, and he lectured widely in Europe, Asia, and Africa.

Commencing in the late 1930s, Lasswell began a long career of service as an advisor to the federal government and to industry and academia as well. His concept of the policy scientist was that of a highly and academically trained expert who uses his or her sophisticated technical knowledge to influence policy in significant ways. To achieve this goal, a scientist, engineer, planner, or other professional must at some point leave his or her narrow career track and move into public administration, citizen advocacy, elective office, or some related policy-making role.

Lasswell's Contribution to the Intellectual Heritage of Public Administration

Lasswell's work is attracting increased interest from scholars seeking to map the intellectual heritage of public administration. Because Lasswell's theoretical concepts are so complex, they have been cited by many authors, in footnotes, without substantive analysis.

Many of Lasswell's ideas have been used by others to such an extent that the original source is often overlooked by readers. A careful perusal of the footnotes in Dror's key works will quickly establish the debt owed to Lasswell. Although Dror's research and writing has fostered the growth of public policy programs in many universities, Dror himself is careful to acknowledge Lasswell's seminal role in developing the public policy concept [2]. Similarly, Edelman's work on symbolism is based largely on Lasswell's concepts [3]. Lasswell's pioneering works on the psychosocial bases of organizational decision making became part of the literature of public administration during the late 1930s. Chester Barnard, writing in the 1930s, and James McCamy and Herbert Simon, writing a decade later, clearly reflect many of Lasswell's ideas. So pervasive did the idea of the psychosocial nature of organizational life become that it is no longer challenged or considered controversial [4].

Another Lasswellian input into the field of public administration consists of his work on the value structure of the environment in which decisions are made and his concept of the decision-making process itself. Both of these theories are central to all administrative activity. On decision making, Lasswell noted that seven power outcomes distinguish the decision-making process: intelligence, promotion, prescription, invocation, application, termination, and appraisal [5].

In regard to values, the environment, and decision making, Lasswell's *A Pre-view of Policy Sciences* systematically presents his view (Ref. 6, p. 22):

At this point it may be helpful to clarify the distinctions between *values* and *institutions*. We defined values by calling attention to culminating events. Institutions, we specified, are the patterns that are relatively specialized to the shaping and sharing of a principal category of values.

Value	Institution
Power	Government, law, political parties
Enlightenment	Languages, mass media, scientific establishments
Wealth	Farms, factories, banks
Well-being	Hospitals, recreational facilities
Skill	Vocational, professional, art schools
Affection	Families, friendship circles
Respect	Social classes and castes
Rectitude	Ethical and religious associations

Institutions refer to the same events that are designated by the value terms; they make it possible to formulate fundamental questions about the interplay between any specific institution and the value-shaping and value-sharing processes which the institution affects, and which it in turn affects. Contextual analysis implies that every institution influences and is in turn influenced by every institution specialized to its value sector, and potentially by every institution in every other sector.

For the many students Lasswell has influenced, these concepts are unique-
ly his. But they also provide a basic underpinning for much that is written
in the public administration field, often without a Lasswellian label.

During and after the years when Lasswell and the writer taught at the
same institution of higher learning, Lasswell displayed a keen interest in
current trends in public administration education and training. He indicated that he viewed the teaching of preservice and in-service students as
an intellectual task of the highest importance. He maintained that academics
had a unique opportunity to influence public policy through the education
and training of public administrators. Values significant to the democratic
process and social change could be transmitted through the mechanisms of
public service education and training.

In 1971, Lasswell described in detail an educational program for policy
scientists. He included suggestions on the use of practitioners as faculty,
the need for faculty with first-hand practical experience, internships, professional placement of graduates, and other practices now institutionalized
in most professional public administration programs (see Ref. 6, pp. 132–
159). Many of his stated concerns are identical to those which have captured
the attention of the National Association of Schools of Public Affairs and
Administration (NASPAA). The NASPAA Standards for Professional
Programs in Master's Degree Programs in Public Affairs/Public Administration treat in prescriptive and in normative terms the issues which Lasswell dealt with in an exploratory fashion.

Lasswell's deep interest in public organizational management encompassed all aspects of the training and career development for future policy
scientists. In describing the role of the policy scientist in a public organization, Lasswell wrote (Ref. 6, pp. 83, 85):

> The career civil servant is not necessarily a policy scientist, although it
> is a great advantage if he has such training and experience. Nor is the
> top officer or political figure necessarily a policy scientist. In the rush of
> things top leaders have little time for most matters; hence they need the
> assistance of those who take a longer view of the situation. . . . A fun-
> damental aim of the policy scientist is to bring about an improved capa-
> bility in the formation and execution of policy.

Lasswell treated many issues central to public administration identity
and education. Lasswell accurately portrayed the ambiguous situation of
Dwight Waldo's "pracademic" (Ref. 6, p. 120):

> The . . . scholar who becomes the mediator between the social environ-
> ment and his colleagues is a target of ambivalent sentiment on the part
> of colleagues and the larger environment, and privately he often shares

the ambivalence. . . . In achieving the new identity it has been necessary to overcome the image of a second-class man of knowledge and a second-class man of action.

Lasswell offered a plan of training for professional public sector managers which included specific university organizational arrangements, student admission requirements, an appropriate prospectus, a model curriculum, an internship program, and a continuing decision seminar (see Ref. 6, pp. 132–142). The seminar, a unique Lasswellian contribution to higher education, was designed to be an ongoing research activity in the form of an academic seminar. A nucleus of participants explores new ideas in a field of common interest over a prolonged period of time. Similar seminars were organized by Lasswell at the many universities at which he taught.

Lasswell was particularly interested in the career problems and development of in-service students. In *A Pre-view of Policy Sciences* Lasswell came dangerously close to writing like an erudite and humane cross between Peter Drucker and Michael Korda. In addition to well-thought-out and managerially relevant statements on the roles of line and staff, the significance and importance of several different kinds of planning, and key factors in organizational design and process, Lasswell was also prone to display his academic wit. Among such concerns, the reader finds such maxims as "short-range success is often the parent of long-range failure" and "if the individual has not learned selective trust as well as selective distrust he is likely to fail." Humorous as these illustrations might be, they also aim directly toward the real world of public administration with which Lasswell was so intimately involved.

Summary

Lasswell's works in the study and analysis of organizational structure and behavior, decision making, education for the public service, policy sciences, and other related topics are reflected throughout the study and practice of public administration today. In this chapter we seek only to begin the search for a more detailed and sustained analysis of the specific ways in which public administration may be defined and developed.

Acknowledgment

The author acknowledges Temple University's Grant in Aid of Research Program for its assistance in support of the collection of data for this chapter.

References

1. See Joseph Goldsen, "Harold Lasswell as Policy Advisor and Consultant," and Heinz Eulau, "HDL is Gone," in *Harold Dwight Lasswell, 1902–1978: In Commemoration and Continuing Commitment*, Yale Law School, Policy Sciences Center, the Ogden Foundation, pp. 78–81 and 88–90.
2. Yehezkel Dror, *Design for Policy Sciences*, American Elsevier, New York, 1971.
3. Murray Edelman, *The Symbolic Uses of Politics*, University of Illinois Press, Urbana, Ill., 1964.
4. Nicholas Henry, *Public Administration and Public Affairs*, Prentice-Hall, Englewood Cliffs, N.J., 1975, p. 34. See also James L. McCamy, "Analysis of the Process of Decision-Making," *Public Administration Review*, 7 (Winter 1947):41–48, and Herbert A. Simon, " A Comment on the Science of Public Administration," *Public Administration Review*, 7 (Summer 1947):200–203.
5. Harold D. Lasswell, *The Signature of Power: Buildings, Communication and Policy*, Transaction Books, New Brunswick, N.J., 1979, p. 86.
6. Harold D. Lasswell, *A Pre-view of Policy Sciences*, American Elsevier, New York, 1971.

Author Index

Subject Index

Action research, 69–72 (*see also* Organization Development)
Administration (*see also* Bureaucracy, Management, Organizations)
  decentralized, 58
  democratic, 56, 67
  principles of, 27, 71
  proverbs of, 27
Administrative agencies: role of production functions, 49–50
Administrative behavior, 115–116
American Political Science Association, 26
American Society for Public Administration, 26
Articles of Confederation, 6
Artifact: use in theory building, 39–41
Artisan: role in theory building, 39–41
Authority relationships
  bureaucratic basis for, 46–47
  iron law of oligarchy, 43–45
  as polycentric order, 48
  as reflection of constitutional

[Authority relationships]
  choice, 48
  rules as artifacts, 42–43

Brownlow Report, 23–24
Bureaucracy (*see also* Administration, Management, Organization)
  authority structures, 65–67
  costs of, 68–69
  impacts on individuals, 65–67
  as positivist science, 69–70
  as reflection of value conflicts, 62
  traditional structures, 57–59
  undercuts democratic values, 63–67
Bureau for Municipal Research, 20–21

Centralization, 58 (*see also* Decentralization)
Checks and balances, 11–13
Classical administration (*see also* Public Administration Theory, Bureaucracy)

[Public administration theory]
   also Public Administration)
behavioralist approach critiqued,
   29
case method, 27
classical foundations of, 6–8, 18–
   24, 27–29
as comparative administration, 28
in democratic framework, 31, 56–
   57
egalitarian trends in, 29–30
European influences upon, 25
as human relations, 27
as neo-classical theory, 10–13, 18,
   24–29
as the "new" public administration, 30, 37n
in a pluralistic context, 27–29
as polycentric democracy, 31, 76
as romantic theory, 8–10, 13–18,
   29–32

Public goods, theory of, 47–48

Romantic administration (*see also*
   Public Administration Theory)
   as community based authority, 17
   as decentralized government, 17
   in a democratic mode, 31
   in the nineteenth century, 13–18
   resurgence in the sixties and seven-
      ties of, 29–32
   as social equity, 30

Social consensus as the objective of
   administration, 13
Social equity, 30
Sovereignty
   definition of, 39
   social orders of, 5
Span of control, 21, 46

Unity of command, 46